absolutely
avocados

For information about permission to reproduce selections from this book, write to Permissions, Houghton Mifflin Harcourt Publishing Company, 215 Park Avenue South, New York, New York 10003.

www.hmhbooks.com

Cover Design: Suzanne Sunwoo

Author Photograph: © Marla Meridith

Interior Design: Joline Rivera

Library of Congress Cataloging-in-Publication Data:

Library of Congress Cataloging-in-Publication Data

Dalkin, Gaby, 1986-
 Absolutely avocados / Gaby Dalkin ; photography by Matt Armendariz.
     pages cm
 Includes index.
  ISBN 978-1-118-41211-4 (cloth : acid-free paper), ISBN 978-1-118-41212-1 (ebk), ISBN 978-1-118-41213-8 (ebk), ISBN 978-1-118-41214-5 (ebk) 1. Cooking (Avocado) I. Title.
  TX813.A9D35 2013
  641.6'4653--dc23

                                                                    2012023283

Printed in China

SZN 10 9 8 7 6 5 4 3 2 1

absolutely
avocados

GABY DALKIN

PHOTOGRAPHY BY MATT ARMENDARIZ

HOUGHTON MIFFLIN HARCOURT

Boston • New York • 2013

contents

acknowledgments

I loved writing this book. It was pretty much my dream cookbook project! I ate approximately 4 pounds of avocados a day for the months that I spent recipe testing, and I loved every last second of it. I could not have done this without a handful of people to whom I owe a huge thank-you!

Thomas, my husband and chief recipe tester, who tasted each and every recipe, until he turned avocado green. You rock.

My sister and best friend, Anya.

Matt Armendariz and Adam C. Pearson, who performed double duty as the brilliant photography and food styling team behind this book and by being two of my best friends.

Dani Fisher, the most glorious prop stylist ever, and Fifty One and a Half for making us custom props and ceramics for the photography.

My editor, Justin Schwartz, who guided me through the entire process and gave me the space to showcase my obsession with avocados, and my agent, Stacey Glick, for working with me throughout the whole book.

Lillian Kang and Laura Bellinger, my trusty recipe testers who tested each and every recipe in this book. They were an absolute pleasure to work with, and I trust them immensely.

All my awesome, fabulous, supportive, and funny What's Gaby Cooking readers. You guys keep me going, and, this book is for you!

My friends, food blogging friends, mentors, and coworkers—you guys know who you are!

And last, my mom and dad for being the most wonderful and encouraging parents in the whole world. I wouldn't be where I am today without your guidance, love, and support.

thank you!

preface

Hi, my name is Gaby, and I love avocados. Yup, it's true. I'm 100 percent avocado obsessed. Addicted. Completely in love. There is rarely a day that goes by that I don't eat avocado in some way, shape, or form.

I grew up in Arizona, which means we ate boatloads of guacamole. When it was on the menu, it was never a question of were we going to order guacamole, but simply a question of how much?

Eventually I wound up in Los Angeles. Looking back, I like to think that this was a strategic decision, since I ended up being so close to many avocado farms and have year-round access to big, beautiful avocados. From there I started my Web site, www.whatsgabycooking.com, and jumped right into the wonderful world of food blogging. After completing culinary school, I started working as a private chef. I love that my life is focused on food and that I get to play in the kitchen each and every day. I've been blessed to work with some phenomenal clients whom I adore. I never in a million years imagined that food blogging would become what it is today, but I love being able to share my favorite recipes with my readers.

I truly enjoy feeding people and bringing my friends and family together for a meal, with avocado of course! I like my food to be simple yet flavorful and not fussy. My cooking style is an eclectic mix of California casual with a Southwest flair and a dash of sass. There is a healthy balance of light and clean food like my Sweet Potato Burgers (page 172) or my Mexican Chopped Salad (page 120) paired with some decadent treats, like Ultimate Nachos (page 97) or Fried Avocado Tacos (page 166).

So, after 419 avocados, many months of recipe testing, and countless days of avocado for breakfast, lunch, dinner, and dessert, I'm so excited to finally share all these mouth watering avocado recipes with you! I hope they find their way into your kitchen and your hearts.

cheers!

everything you need to know about **avocados**

types of avocados

There are hundreds of avocado varieties all over the world. And while the Hass is most commonly known and used, there are a few other varieties you should know about.

The **Hass** avocado is the most common of all avocados. It's produced year-round in different climates that support avocado growth. This avocado has a dark, bumpy skin and darkens to a purplish black color as it ripens.

The **Fuerte** avocado has a much different skin from that of the Hass. It's a lighter green color and much smoother. This avocado will stay green, rather than darkening, as it ripens. Fuertes have a rich and creamy flesh and are harvested in late fall through early spring. If you find a Fuerte, be sure to pick it up. It's one of my favorites!

The **Gwen** avocado is similar in appearance to the Hass but with smaller bumps on the skin. This avocado will darken as it ripens, like the Hass. The Gwen has a creamy golden flesh when cut open.

The Bacon avocado is a late fall to early spring varietal and has a smooth, thin, green skin. The Bacon has a rich and creamy flavor, although it's not quite as oily as other avocados, and also has quite a large pit.

The **Pinkerton** avocado has a rough, pebble-like skin and a slightly rich and nutty taste. Pinkertons are great because they have relatively small pits and thus will have a more useful fruit-to-seed ratio.

The Nabal avocado is a large, round, softball-shaped avocado. It has a greenish gold flesh and a hard skin that looks like it has freckles. Nabal avocados are hard to come by and quite expensive, but the expense is totally worth it if you can find one.

The **Zutano** avocado closely resembles the Fuerte avocado yet isn't looked upon as highly since it yields a less rich and creamy flesh. It has a clean and mellow flavor but can sometimes be a touch fibrous.

how to...

how to buy an avocado

When shopping for avocados at the market, you want to look for those without any dark spots or blemishes. If you want to use the fruit immediately, look for darker green avocados that are firm but give slightly under pressure. You do not want a mushy avocado, as this is a sign of overripening. If you don't want to use the avocados for a few days, look for brighter green fruit that feels firm. They will turn a darker green color as they continue to ripen.

how to store an avocado

If you buy an avocado that needs a few days to ripen, go ahead and gently put it in a brown paper bag. Store the bag at room temperature and the avocado will ripen within a few days. If you want the avocado to ripen quickly, add an apple or a banana to the bag. This introduces ethylene gas, which causes the avocado to ripen even faster.

If you buy an avocado that is already ripe but you need to store it for a day or two, keep the avocado in the fridge until you are ready to use it. Be aware, however, that keeping a ripe avocado in the fridge for more than 2 or 3 days will cause it to brown.

If you need to store a cut avocado, sprinkle the exposed flesh with lemon juice, lime juice, or white vinegar and place a piece of plastic wrap around the avocado to ensure that no air gets in. Refrigerate the wrapped avocado for up to 2 days.

health benefits

Avocados are a nutrient-dense fruit that have numerous health benefits and contain the following: monounsaturated fats, vitamin K, folate, potassium, vitamin E, lutein, magnesium, vitamin C, and vitamin B6. You might be asking yourself, Why do I want to eat a fruit with monounsaturated fats? Well, these are actually good fats. Monounsaturated fats are better for your health than saturated or trans fats. Studies have found that eating foods that are rich in monounsaturated fats can improve blood cholesterol levels by lowering your LDL (bad cholesterol) and increasing your HDL (good cholesterol).

Using avocado as a substitute for butter or mayonnaise drastically cuts down on calories, too. Two tablespoons of avocado has 50 calories, while 2 tablespoons of butter has 204 calories and 2 tablespoons of mayonnaise has 109 calories. Avocados also have no cholesterol or sodium, unlike both butter and mayonnaise.

how to cut an avocado

1. Hold a sharp knife in your dominant hand and the avocado in your other hand. Using the knife, cut the avocado in half lengthwise around the pit starting at the narrower end. 2. Holding the avocado in the palm of your hand, use your other hand to twist and pull the two halves of the avocado apart. 3. Expose the avocado pit. 4. Using your knife, firmly tap the pit so that the knife wedges itself into the pit. Gently twist the knife with the pit attached so that the pit easily comes out of the avocado. Discard the pit. 5. From this point, there are two ways to cut the avocado. Option 1 (I prefer this way for guacamole and any other recipe where the avocado is going to be mashed up): Score the avocado in a crosshatch pattern. 6. Using a large spoon, scoop the avocado flesh out of the avocado skin and transfer to a bowl. 7. Option 2 (I prefer this method when the avocado is going to stand front and center on a dish, since this method allows for a cleaner cut): Once you have removed the pit, place the avocado, flat side down, on a cutting board. Cut the avocado in half lengthwise. 8. Gently peel back the avocado skin. 9. Cut the avocado in a crosshatch pattern or thinly slice depending on your preference.

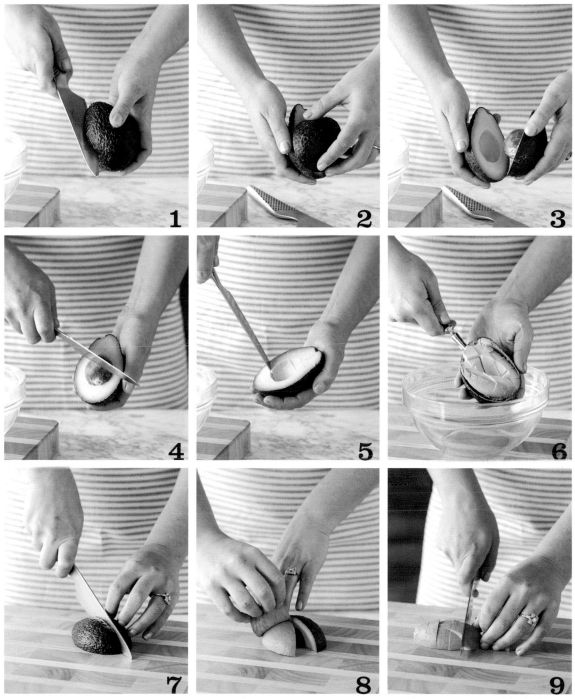

breakfast

Avocados for breakfast just make perfect sense. They can take on a variety of ingredients and enhance the entire meal. Avocado toast is my go-to morning meal when I'm in a rush, but if I have more time to make a leisurely breakfast, I will happily whip up any of these recipes that feature avocado. I don't quite remember when I started eating avocado for breakfast, but let's be honest here, I'm so glad that I do!

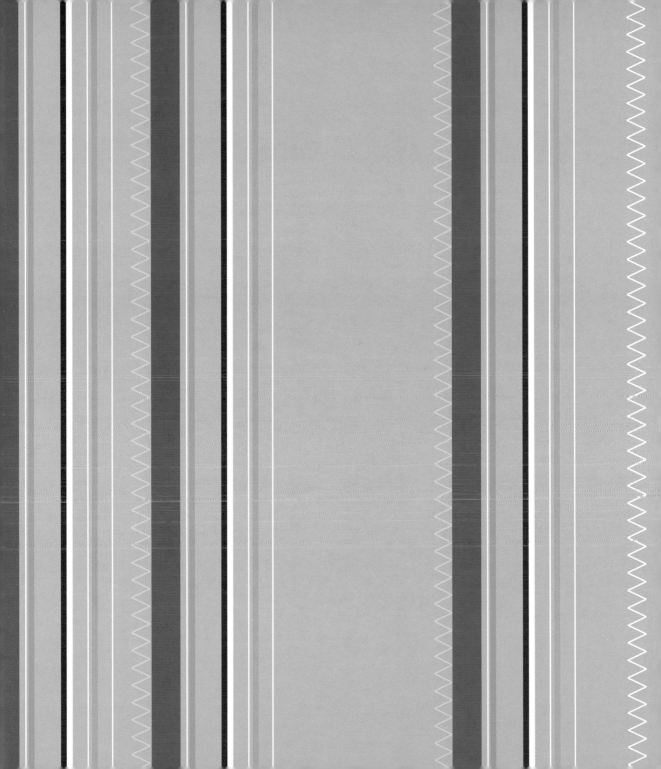

avocado & chorizo breakfast hash

Mexican chorizo is my jam. I add it to a ton of dishes when I'm in the kitchen, but my favorite use of this chorizo is in my avocado breakfast hash. The smoky and spicy notes of the chorizo play perfectly with the avocado and roasted potatoes, and together it wakes you right up in the morning!

Prep Time: 10 minutes
Cook Time: 35 minutes
Total Time: 45 minutes
Serves: 4

1   pound red skinned potatoes
3   tablespoon extra-virgin olive
    oil, divided
    Coarse salt and freshly
    ground black pepper to taste
5   ounces Mexican chorizo
    sausage, removed from
    casing (found in the
    Hispanic refrigerated
    section of your market)
1   red bell pepper
1   medium yellow onion
1   tablespoon finely chopped
    garlic
1   Hass avocado
2   tablespoons finely chopped
    fresh chives, for garnish

Preheat the oven to 425°F.

Scrub the potatoes under water to remove any dirt. Cut the potatoes in $\frac{1}{2}$-inch cubes. Transfer the potatoes onto a non-stick baking sheet, drizzle with 2 tablespoons of olive oil, season with salt and pepper, and toss with your hands to combine. Make sure the potatoes are in a single layer on the baking sheet, transfer to the oven and bake for 30 to 40 minutes, until they are tender and done, tossing every 15 minutes to ensure they are evenly cooked.

While the potatoes are in the oven, put a large heavy bottom skillet over medium heat and add the remaining tablespoon of olive oil. Add the Mexican chorizo to the skillet and break up with a wooden spoon. Cook, stirring and breaking up the chorizo, until it is browned and crisp, about 10 minutes. Using a slotted spoon, remove the chorizo from the skillet and set aside. The chorizo will have left some fat in the skillet; leave the fat there for the vegetables.

Remove the seeds and ribs of the red bell pepper and cut the pepper and yellow onion in $\frac{1}{2}$-inch cubes. Transfer these vegetables back to the same heavy bottom skillet along with the leftover fat from the chorizo. If there isn't enough fat in the pan, drizzle a few teaspoons of olive oil over the vegetables. Cook the vegetables over medium heat, stirring, until the onions are translucent, about 5 minutes. Add the garlic and cook, stirring for about 1 minute more. Turn off the heat.

Once the potatoes are cooked, remove them from the oven and transfer them to the skillet with the vegetables. Return the chorizo to the pan. Turn the heat to medium and toss to combine. Cook for 2 to 3 additional minutes.

Cut the avocado in half lengthwise. Remove the pit from the avocado and discard. Remove the avocado from the skin, and place the avocado flesh on a cutting board. Cut the avocado in $\frac{1}{2}$-inch cubes and transfer the avocado to the skillet. Toss everything together and turn off the heat. Sprinkle the chives over the hash and season with salt and pepper and serve.

avocado toast

If I had to pick one breakfast to have for the rest of my life, well, this avocado toast would win hands down. Once upon a time when avocados were on sale for mere pennies, I bought about twenty (mind you, I lived by myself) and then was faced with the fact that I needed to eat them basically for breakfast, lunch, and dinner. So mashing up avocado and spreading it onto a piece of toast seemed like a perfectly reasonable thing to do. Best breakfast ever! Especially when you're on the go!

Prep Time: 3 minutes
Cook Time: 2 minutes
Total Time: 5 minutes
Serves: 2

1   Hass avocado
2   pieces sliced French bread (or any other toast-like bread that you prefer)
½   teaspoon coarse salt
1   lemon

Cut the avocado in half lengthwise. Remove the pit from the avocado and discard. Remove the avocado from the skin, and transfer the avocado flesh to medium bowl. Using a fork, mash the avocado until it's half chunky and half smooth.

Put the 2 pieces of toast in a toaster or toaster oven and toast for 2 to 3 minutes until just lightly golden brown and crisp. Remove the pieces of bread from the toaster and transfer each to a plate. Spread ½ of the avocado mixture on each piece of toast. Sprinkle the salt on top of each layer of avocado and finish with a small squeeze of lemon juice. Enjoy immediately.

avocado crème fraîche egg scramble

There are three secrets to the ultimate scrambled eggs. The first is cooking your eggs very slowly and allowing them to form ribbons rather than quickly scrambling and whisking everything together. The second is crème fraîche. It's thick, rich, and creamy, and you'll basically never want to have scrambled eggs without it again. And the third secret is avocados!

Prep Time: 5 minutes
Cook Time: 5 minutes
Total Time: 10 minutes
Serves: 2

6 large eggs
2 tablespoons butter
2 tablespoons crème fraîche
1 tablespoon finely snipped fresh chives
½ Haas avocado
   Coarse salt and freshly ground black pepper
2 pieces toasted whole wheat bread

Crack the eggs in a medium sized bowl and whisk together.

Add the butter to a 9-inch non-stick skillet over medium heat. Let the butter start to melt and add the eggs. Using a spatula, continue to stir the eggs over medium heat; you want the eggs to cook slowly, so it's helpful the keep the eggs constantly moving. Once the eggs start to scramble, add the crème fraîche and stir to combine. Remove the eggs from the heat before they look completely done. Finish stirring and let the eggs continue to cook using the heat of the skillet but not over the stove. Add the snipped chives and stir.

Cut the avocado in half lengthwise. Remove the pit from the avocado and discard. Remove the avocado from the skin, place the avocado on a cutting board, and cut in thin slices. Transfer the avocado slices on top of the soft scrambled eggs.

Season with salt and pepper and serve immediately with toast.

huevos rancheros with chipotle salsa & avocado

If you've got 30 minutes, then huevos rancheros might just be your new most favorite way to start the day. Freshly fried tortillas topped with homemade chipotle salsa, a perfect fried egg, some creamy avocado, and queso fresco to boot? Yes, please! I'll take seconds, and thirds. These huevos rancheros are my go-to when preparing brunch for a crowd.

Prep Time: 15 minutes
Cook Time: 15 minutes
Total Time: 30 minutes
Serves: 6
Sauce yield: 2 cups

1   14-ounce can fire roasted tomatoes
⅓ cup chopped yellow onion
¼ cup chopped fresh cilantro
1 to 2 canned chipotle pepper in adobo sauce, seeds removed and chopped, plus 1 tablespoon of the liquid from the can
Juice of 1 lime
1   jalapeño, split in half and seeds removed
2   garlic cloves
1   teaspoon coarse salt
1   teaspoon freshly ground black pepper
¼ cup grapeseed oil (or vegetable oil)
6   corn tortillas
1   14-ounce can of warm refried beans
2   tablespoons butter
6   large eggs
1   Hass avocado
½ cup grated queso fresco
Coarse salt and freshly ground black pepper to taste

Add the fire roasted tomatoes, onion, cilantro, chipotle peppers and their liquid, lime juice, jalapeño, garlic, salt, and pepper to a food processor bowl. Pulse for 1 to 2 minutes until smooth. Adjust the salt and pepper if needed. Transfer the salsa to a bowl and set aside.

Heat the grapeseed oil in a large skillet over medium high heat until shimmering. Add the corn tortillas, 2 at a time, and fry for 60 to 90 seconds on each side until golden brown and crisp. Remove the tortillas from the oil and transfer to a paper-towel lined plate to dry. Repeat this process for the remaining tortillas. Smear ¼ cup of the warmed refried beans onto each tortilla and add ¼ cup of the chipotle salsa.

Once the tortillas have been fried, drain the oil from the skillet and put the butter into the skillet to melt. Carefully crack 3 eggs in the skillet, evenly spaced so they have room to cook, and cook until the egg white is solid, 3 to 4 minutes. Remove the fried eggs from the skillet and lay each one onto a tortilla. Repeat this process for the remaining 3 eggs.

Cut the avocado in half lengthwise. Remove the pit from the avocado and discard. Remove the avocado from the skin, and place the avocado on a cutting board. Cut 6 thin slices from each half of the avocado and transfer 2 slices on top of each fried egg. Sprinkle the queso fresco on top and season with salt and pepper if desired. Serve immediately.

southwestern egg casserole

This large casserole stuffed with cheese, avocado, tomatoes, beans, and a few other fun foods is a great way to serve a crowd. Plus, it's the perfect way to use up any leftovers in the fridge from the past week's meals. Have a few extra beans from taco night? Throw them in! Leftover scallions from another night are perfect. It all makes sense in this baked egg casserole.

Prep Time: 10 minutes
Cook Time: 45 minutes
Total Time: 55 minutes
Serves: 9

8   large eggs
½   cup 2% low-fat milk
3   ounces cotija cheese (feta
      cheese may be substituted)
¾   teaspoons coarse salt
½   teaspoon freshly ground
      black pepper
1   Hass avocado
1   cup halved cherry tomatoes
½   cup canned black beans,
      drained and rinsed
3   tablespoons canned diced
      green chiles
¼   cup snipped green onions,
      green parts only
1   tablespoon minced jalapeño

Preheat the oven to 350°F.

Crack the eggs in a medium sized bowl and whisk together with the milk, cotija cheese, salt, and pepper. Set aside.

Spray a medium sized baking dish (enough to hold 1 quart) with non-stick cooking spray.

Cut the avocado in half lengthwise. Remove the pit from the avocado and discard. Remove the avocado from the skin, place the avocado on a cutting board, and cut in 1-inch dice. Add ¾ of the avocado to the egg mixture, reserving a few pieces to top the casserole with. Set aside 2 tablespoons of cherry tomatoes, 2 tablespoons of black beans, 1 tablespoon diced green chiles, 1 tablespoon green onions, and 1 teaspoon jalapeños and add the rest to the egg mixture.

Pour the mixture in the prepared baking pan. Bake for 45 minutes, until the center just springs back when touched. You don't want the eggs to be overcooked, but you want them to stay moist and fluffy. Sprinkle the reserved ingredients on top and cut into 9 evenly sized pieces and serve.

poached eggs over avocado & smoked salmon

Every few months I like to have all my food industry friends over for brunch. It's basically an excuse to have everyone bring something over to eat, and that way I'm not stuck cooking for ten. Each time I'm consistently amazed by what my friends create, but this particular breakfast item was inspired by my friend Lucy Lean, a fellow food blogger and author here in LA. She made the simplest breakfast of microgreens, poached eggs, and smoked salmon. It knocked my socks off, and I've been making it ever since… with the addition of avocado, of course!

Prep Time: 10 minutes
Cook Time: 35 minutes
Total Time: 45 minutes
Serves: 4

1   tablespoon white vinegar
2   cups microgreens
1   Meyer lemon, or regular lemons
8   ounces smoked salmon
1   Hass avocado
4   large eggs
    Coarse salt and freshly ground black pepper to taste

Fill a shallow pan with at least 3 inches of water. Add the white vinegar; bring the water to a boil and then reduce to a simmer.

Equally divide the microgreens among 4 small plates. Squeeze a touch of lemon juice on each pile of greens.

Lay 2 ounces of the smoked salmon on top of the greens.

Cut the avocado in half lengthwise. Remove the pit from the avocado and discard. Remove the avocado from the skin, place the avocado on a cutting board, and cut into thin slices. Put the avocado slices on top of the smoked salmon and add another squeeze of lemon juice.

Crack an egg into a small prep bowl. Carefully slip the egg from the prep bowl into the poaching water. With a spoon, nudge the egg white together so the egg remains as close together as possible. Repeat this for the remaining 3 eggs. Cover the pan with a tight-fitting lid and turn off the heat. Let the eggs cook for 3 to 4 minutes, then carefully remove each egg with a slotted spoon, letting any excess water drip off. Transfer the egg to the top of the avocado and smoked salmon.

Season with salt and pepper and serve immediately.

avocado quiche lorraine

I love quiche. The flaky and buttery crust is so good that I could basically eat it on its own. But give me a quiche with avocado and Gruyère and you won't hear a peep out of me for a while. Because clearly, I'll be eating.

Prep Time: 10 minutes
Cook Time: 30 minutes
Total Time: 1 hour
(including cooling)
Serves: 8

1 piece store-bought pie dough, enough for a 9-inch pie dish (roughly 8 ounces)
4 large eggs
1 cup 2% milk
⅓ cup heavy cream
  Coarse salt and freshly ground black pepper
  Pinch of freshly grated nutmeg
1 cup shredded Gruyère cheese
½ cup cubed cooked ham
2 tablespoons snipped fresh chives
1 Hass avocado

Preheat the oven to 350°F.

Roll the pie dough out on a floured surface to an 11-inch circle.

Line a 9-inch pie dish with the prepared pie dough and crimp the edges with your fingers. Lay a sheet of parchment paper over the dough and fill the pie with pie weights or dried beans. Blind bake the pie crust for 10 to 12 minutes until the pie crust is lightly golden. Remove the crust from oven and let cool. Once cooled, remove the pie weights or dried beans and parchment paper and set aside for another use.

In a large bowl, whisk together the eggs, milk, and heavy cream. Season the mixture with salt, pepper, and nutmeg. Add the grated Gruyère cheese and cubed ham along with the snipped chives.

Cut the avocado in half lengthwise. Remove the pit from the avocado and discard. Remove the avocado from the skin, and place it on a cutting board. Cut the avocado into thin strips and lay them on the bottom of the cooled pie crust.

Pour the egg mixture over the avocado. Bake for 30 to 35 minutes, until the egg mixture has set. Remove from the oven and let cool. Slice and serve.

migas

I can't believe that I didn't have migas until I was 23! For someone who grew up in Arizona and frequently headed down to Mexico for spring break and summer vacation, I was clearly living under a rock. Not only are migas another one of my favorite breakfast items, but they are also the perfect cure if you had a little too much to drink the night before, if you know what I mean.

Prep Time: 10 minutes
Cook Time: 12 minutes
Total Time: 22 minutes
Serves: 8

3   corn tortillas
¼   cup vegetable oil
8   large eggs
¼   cup 2% milk
2   tablespoons butter
½   cup chopped tomatoes
¼   cup canned diced green chiles
½   cup grated pepper Jack cheese
¼   cup chopped fresh cilantro
1   cup store-bought pico de gallo
1   Hass avocado
    Coarse salt and freshly
      ground black pepper to taste

Cut the corn tortillas into 1-inch squares.

Heat the vegetable oil in a large skillet over medium-high heat. When the oil begins to shimmer, add the tortilla squares and fry until just crisp, about 30 seconds on each side. Remove the crisp tortillas with a slotted spoon and driain on a paper towel–lined plate.

In a large bowl, whisk together the eggs and milk. In another large skillet, melt the butter over medium-high heat. Add the tomatoes and green chiles and cook, stirring, for 1 minute. Add the crisp tortillas to the skillet and stir to combine. Reduce the heat to medium low and pour in the egg mixture. Continually stir the egg mixture until the eggs are just soft but scrambled. Add the cheese and cilantro and stir to combine. Remove the migas from the skillet and transfer to a serving platter. Top the migas with the pico de gallo.

Cut the avocado in half lengthwise. Remove the pit from the avocado and discard. Remove the avocado from the skin, place the avocado on a cutting board, and cut into thin strips. Arrange the thinly sliced avocado on top of the migas. Season with salt and pepper and serve immediately.

did you know?

Another name for the avocado is the "alligator pear," so-called because of its alligator skin texture & pear shape.

avocado super food smoothie

Avocado in a smoothie? Why not? This smoothie, packed with super foods left and right, also is super-creamy because of the addition of avocado. It's the perfect grab-and-go breakfast when you're on the move.

Prep Time: 5 minutes
Total Time: 5 minutes
Serves: 2

1 Hass avocado
1 cup frozen blueberries, plus more as needed
1 cup fresh blueberries
15 mint leaves
1½ cups organic orange juice
¼ cup plain yogurt, plus more as needed
2 tablespoons agave nectar or honey
½ cup frozen raspberries (optional)

Cut the avocados in half lengthwise. Remove the pit from the avocado and discard. Remove the avocado from the skin, and place the avocado flesh in a blender.

Add the frozen blueberries, fresh blueberries, mint, orange juice, yogurt, agave nectar, and raspberries to the blender. Blend the ingredients together for 1 to 2 minutes, until completely smooth. Add more orange juice if the consistency is too thick, or more frozen blueberries if you want a slushier texture. Serve immediately.

Note: I typically don't add ice since I use frozen blueberries, but you can add a handful of ice if you want an even slushier texture.

guacamole

I've been a guacamole addict for most of my life. Enjoying it is basically an everyday occurrence for me, and I find a way to sneak it into just about every meal possible. It wasn't always like that, though; in fact, it was quite the contrary. We moved to Arizona when I was five years old and while I don't remember this, my parents love reminding me about our first Mexican restaurant experience. My entire extended family was in town helping us get settled into our new home, and we took everyone out for dinner at one of the most popular Mexican restaurants in Tucson. I was quite the happy little girl until the server put a bowl of guacamole on our table, at which point I started crying and telling anyone who would listen about my dislike for guacamole. About 47 seconds after that started, my mom made me try a bite, and the rest is pretty much history. Not only was I completely embarrassed about how I had acted, but I also then proceeded to eat the entire bowl of guacamole by myself. And now, twenty some years later, I am a guacamole fanatic who will eat guacamole for breakfast, lunch, and dinner without a second thought!

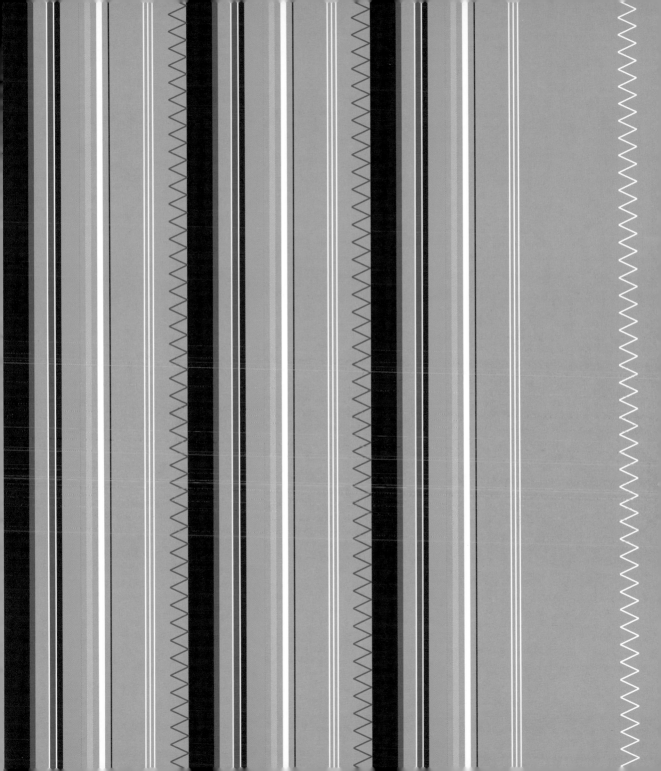

charred corn guacamole

It's true. I'm a total guacamole freak. I'll order it at every restaurant and grab a bite at any party. It's my favorite dish and I can't imagine life without it. This charred corn guacamole is perfect for a summertime soirée. The corn provides a fun little pop when you scoop up a pile of guacamole on a freshly fried tortilla chip!

Prep Time: 10 minutes
Cook Time: 15 minutes
Total Time: 25 minutes
Serves: 4

2 ears of corn, husks and silks removed

2 teaspoons extra-virgin olive oil

3 Hass avocados

⅓ cup chopped scallions

1 tablespoon fresh lemon juice

1 teaspoon ground cumin

½ teaspoon red pepper flakes

Coarse salt and freshly ground black pepper to taste

Tortilla chips, for serving

Prepare a gas, charcoal, or indoor grill.

Brush the cleaned ears of corn with the olive oil and transfer them directly to your grill. Let the corn start to blister for a few minutes on each side, rotating accordingly until all sides of the corn are slightly charred, about 10 minutes. Remove the corn from the grill and let cool.

Cut the kernels off the cobs by laying each cob flat on a cutting board and using a sharp knife to remove the kernels. Transfer the kernels to a large bowl. Set aside a handful to garnish the guacamole.

Cut each avocado in half lengthwise. Remove the pit from the avocado and discard. Remove the avocado from the skin, and place the avocado flesh in the bowl.

Add the scallions, lemon juice, cumin, red pepper flakes, salt, and pepper. Mash with a fork until halfway smooth and creamy. Taste and add more salt and pepper if desired.

Serve immediately with tortilla chips.

chipotle guacamole

This creamy guacamole is perfectly complemented with the smoky notes of chipotle chiles in adobo sauce. You can spice up this guacamole with extra chipotle if you're a spice lover, or you can just add 1 chipotle pepper to give you a nice mellow smoky finish.

Prep Time: 5 minutes
Total Time: 5 minutes
Serves: 4

3 Hass avocados
⅓ cup chopped fresh cilantro
1 tablespoon fresh lime juice
   1 or 2 canned chipotle chile peppers in adobo sauce, chopped, plus 1 to 2 teaspoons of the sauce from the can
Coarse salt and freshly ground black pepper to taste
Tortilla chips, for serving

Cut each avocado in half lengthwise. Remove the pit from the avocado and discard. Remove the avocado from the skin, and place the avocado flesh in a bowl.

Add the cilantro, lime juice, chipotle pepper, adobo sauce, salt, and pepper to the bowl. Mash with a fork until half smooth and half chunky. Taste and add more adobo or salt and pepper if desired.

Serve immediately with tortilla chips.

mango & cilantro guacamole

Mangos are not just for snacking and cocktails. I mean, don't get me wrong, I love a mango margarita as much as the next girl, but finely chopped mangos make for a perfect addition to a guacamole. Plus, the mango gives this guacamole a bright color that just makes you want to throw a party!

Prep Time: 10 minutes
Total Time: 10 minutes
Serves: 4

3 Hass avocados
1 ripe mango
⅓ cup chopped fresh cilantro
¼ cup chopped red onion
1 serrano chile pepper, seeded
   and finely chopped
1 tablespoon fresh lime juice
   Coarse salt and freshly
   ground black pepper to taste
   Tortilla chips, for serving

Cut each avocado in half lengthwise. Remove the pit from the avocado and discard. Remove the avocado from the skin, and place the avocado flesh in a bowl.

Using a vegetable peeler, remove the skin of the mango. Using a sharp knife, slice the wide flat part of the fruit off one side of the pit. Repeat this process for the other side of the mango. Transfer the 2 mango slices to a cutting board and cut into ½-inch pieces.

Add the mango, cilantro, red onion, chile, lime juice, salt, and pepper to the bowl. Mash with a fork until half smooth and half chunky. Taste and add more salt and pepper if desired.

Serve immediately with tortilla chips.

bacon-cotija guacamole

Bacon. Cotija. Avocado. Could you really ask for anything more? It's not fair to ask me to choose my favorite guacamole—it would be like asking a parent to choose their favorite child. But I'll tell you this: Bacon-Cotija Guacamole and I, well, we get along really well!

Prep Time: 5 minutes
Cook Time: 25 to 30 minutes
Total Time: 30 to 35 minutes
Serves: 4

4 strips bacon (I prefer uncured applewood-smoked bacon)
3 Hass avocados
½ cup chopped fresh cilantro
½ cup crumbled cotija cheese, plus more if desired
1 tablespoon finely chopped serrano chile pepper
Juice of 1 lime
Coarse salt and freshly ground black pepper to taste
Tortilla chips, for serving

Preheat the oven to 400°F.

Line a baking sheet with aluminum foil. Lay the bacon on the baking sheet in a single layer and transfer to the oven. Let the bacon cook for 20 to 25 minutes, until just crispy, turning the bacon over once in the middle of the cooking time. Remove the baking sheet from the oven and transfer the bacon to a paper towel–lined plate to cool. Once the bacon is cool enough to touch, chop it into bite-size pieces and set aside.

Cut each avocado in half lengthwise. Remove the pit from the avocado and discard. Remove the avocado from the skin, and place the avocado flesh in a bowl.

Add the cilantro, cotija cheese, serrano pepper, lime juice, salt, and pepper to the bowl. Mash with a fork until half smooth and half chunky. Fold in half of the bacon. Taste and add more salt and pepper if desired. Garnish the guacamole with the remaining bacon, and add more crumbled cotija cheese if desired.

Serve immediately with tortilla chips.

did you know?

Spanish explorers could not pronounce *ahuacatl*, so they called the avocado *aguacate*. This is the origin of the word *guacamole*.

spicy sesame guacamole

Sesame rice crackers are one of my latest obsessions. So it was only fair that I should develop a guacamole to pair perfectly with these crackers. The ginger and garlic sauce are unexpected but welcome flavors that make this guacamole perfect for any Asian-inspired meal.

Prep Time: 15 minutes
Total Time: 15 minutes
Serves: 4

3   Hass avocados
⅓   cup chopped red onion
¼   cup thinly sliced scallions,
       white and light green parts
       only
1   tablespoon fresh lime juice
2   teaspoons chili-garlic sauce
1½   teaspoons soy sauce
1   teaspoon grated fresh ginger
1½   teaspoons black sesame seeds
½   teaspoon toasted sesame oil
       Coarse salt and freshly
       ground black pepper to taste
       (optional)
       Sesame rice crackers, for
       serving

Cut each avocado in half lengthwise. Remove the pit from the avocado and discard. Remove the avocado from the skin, and place the avocado flesh in a bowl.

Add the red onion, scallions, lime juice, chili-garlic sauce, soy sauce, ginger, 1 teaspoon of the sesame seeds, and the sesame oil. Mash with a fork until half smooth and half chunky. Taste and add salt and pepper if desired. Sprinkle with the remaining ½ teaspoon sesame seeds.

Serve immediately with sesame rice crackers.

cajun shrimp guacamole

Don't get me wrong. I love scooping up my fresh guacamole with freshly fried tortilla chips, but how about a fun little spin on your guacamole? After returning home from a trip to New Orleans, I was cooking up shrimp left and right and at one point randomly dipped one into a batch of guacamole. It was perfection. The juicy and seasoned shrimp is a nice change from the typical crunch of a tortilla chip.

Prep Time: 10 minutes
Cook Time: 10 minutes
Total Time: 20 minutes
Serves: 4

4   tablespoons (½ stick) butter
1   tablespoon Cajun seasoning
1   pound medium shrimp,
      peeled and deveined
    Coarse salt and freshly
      ground black pepper to taste
3   Hass avocados
⅓   cup chopped red bell pepper
½   cup thinly sliced scallions
¼   cup finely chopped yellow
      onion
    Zest of 1 lemon
1   tablespoon fresh lemon juice

Combine 2 tablespoons of the butter and ½ tablespoon of the Cajun seasoning in a large skillet over high heat. Allow the spice to bloom for about 1 minute, and then add ½ of the shrimp and cook until the shrimp is pink and fully cooked, about 2 minutes on each side. Season the shrimp with salt and pepper. Remove the shrimp from the skillet and set aside to rest and cool to room temperature. Repeat this process with the remaining butter, Cajun seasoning, and shrimp.

Cut each avocado in half lengthwise. Remove the pit from the avocado and discard. Remove the avocado from the skin, and place the avocado flesh in a bowl.

Add the red bell pepper, scallions, onion, lemon zest, lemon juice, salt, and pepper to the bowl. Mash with a fork until half smooth and half chunky. Taste and add more salt and pepper if desired.

Serve immediately with the shrimp for dipping.

goat cheese guacamole

I have a tendency to always buy goat cheese when I shop, and then all of a sudden there will be four or five blocks of goat cheese sitting in my fridge. Lucky for me, and you if you have a similar problem, this guacamole basically saves the day. Not to mention it will probably change your life. The goat cheese gives the guacamole an even creamier texture and the perfect tang. It's almost impossible to show any self-control with this one!

Prep Time: 5 minutes
Total Time: 5 minutes
Serves: 4

3 Hass avocados
⅓ cup crumbled goat cheese
¼ cup chopped fresh chives
¼ cup chopped sun-dried
  tomatoes in oil
1 tablespoon fresh lemon juice
  Coarse salt and freshly
    ground black pepper to taste
  Tortilla chips, for serving

Cut each avocado in half lengthwise. Remove the pit from the avocado and discard. Remove the avocado from the skin, and place the avocado flesh in a bowl.

Add the goat cheese, chives, sun-dried tomatoes, lemon juice, salt, and pepper. Mash with a fork until half smooth and creamy. Taste and add more salt and pepper if desired.

Serve immediately with tortilla chips.

roasted poblano & caramelized onion guacamole

Poblano peppers, also known as pasilla peppers, are mild chiles that, when roasted, provide an awesome flavor to this guacamole. Pair that flavor combo with some deeply caramelized onions and you'll realize that this is an addictive guacamole that you can't quite get enough of.

Prep Time: 10 minutes
Cooking Time: 1 hour 5 minutes
Total Time: 1 hour 15 minutes
Serves: 4

1 medium yellow onion
2 tablespoons extra-virgin olive oil
Coarse salt to taste
1 large poblano chile pepper
3 Hass avocados
¼ cup chopped fresh chives
Juice of 1 lime
Freshly ground black pepper to taste
Tortilla chips, for serving

Cut the onion in half from root to top. Remove the skin from the onion and discard. Cut the onion into ¼-inch dice.

Add the olive oil to a large heavy skillet. Heat over medium-high heat until the oil shimmers. Add the diced onion and stir until evenly coated with oil. Reduce the heat to medium-low and cook, stirring every few minutes to ensure no burning. After about 10 minutes, sprinkle ½ teaspoon of salt over the onions. Let the onions cook until a dark brown color but not burned, 30 to 35 minutes. You might need to turn the heat down to low toward the end of the cooking process. If the onions are sticking to the bottom of the pan, add a few teaspoons of water and scrape up the browned bits on the bottom. Transfer the caramelized onions to a bowl.

To roast the poblano pepper, turn a gas burner on high heat. Put the poblano pepper directly over the flame and let it char for a few minutes on each side, until the skin is black and blistered. Once one side of the skin is bubbly, rotate the pepper with a pair of kitchen tongs to finish the remaining sides of the poblano pepper. Alternatively, if you have an electric stove, you can roast the peppers in your oven. Turn the oven to broil and place the poblano pepper on a baking sheet. Place the baking sheet into the oven and let the pepper blacken under the broiler. Once the skin is charred, after 8 to 10 minutes, put the pepper in a large zip-top plastic bag, and let it sit zipped in the bag for 20 minutes. This will allow the pepper to steam and will make removing the skin much easier. After 20 minutes, use your fingers to pull off the skin and then rinse the pepper under cool water. Slice the top off the pepper and discard. Cut the pepper in half lengthwise and discard the seeds. Dice the pepper in ¼-inch dice and transfer to the bowl with the onions.

Cut each avocado in half lengthwise. Remove the pit from the avocado and discard. Remove the avocado from the skin, and place the avocado flesh in the bowl with the caramelized onions and roasted poblano pepper. Add the chives, lime juice, ¾ teaspoon salt, and ½ teaspoon black pepper to the mixture.

Mash with a fork until half smooth and half chunky. Taste and add more salt and pepper if desired.

Serve immediately with tortilla chips.

"Pair that flavor combo with some deeply caramelized onions and you'll realize that this is an addictive guacamole that you can't quite get enough of."

dips & sauces

I am as obsessed with avocado in a dip or a sauce as I am with it in guacamole. I'll throw avocados into salsa on a regular basis and add it to dips and sauces to enhance my meals. All the dips and sauces in this chapter are super easy to make and can be used in a variety of ways. You can serve these dips with some fresh lightly salted tortilla chips, or serve them over a grilled piece of protein, or toss some into a salad, or use one on a sandwich! The possibilities are endless.

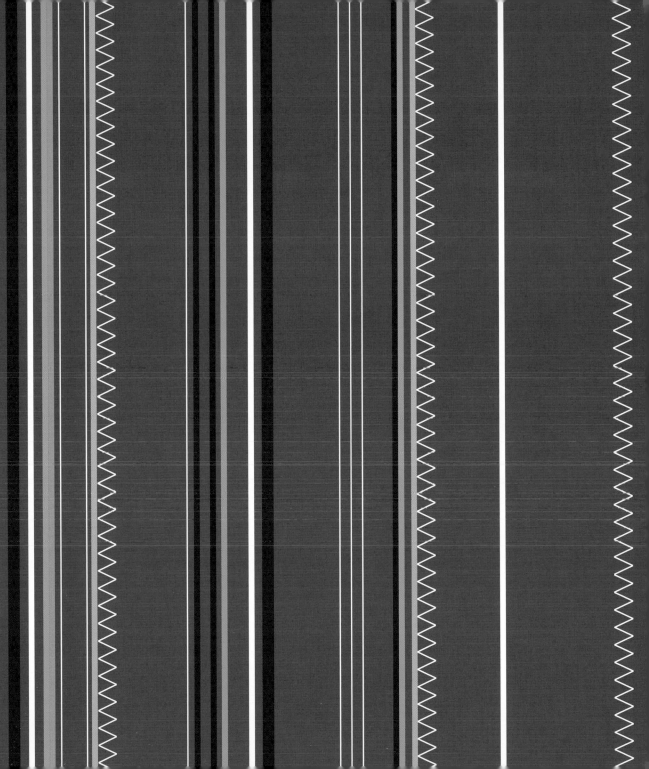

tomatillo-avocado salsa

Hands down, this is the best tomatillo salsa in the entire world. The tart flavor from tomatillos is perfectly complemented by the creaminess of the avocado. You'll want to make a double batch of this salsa, because you'll be adding it to every savory dish for days!

Prep Time: 5 minutes
Cook Time: 20 minutes
Total Time: 25 minutes
Serves: 6 to 8 (about 3 cups)

6   medium tomatillos
1   tablespoon extra-virgin olive oil
2   Hass avocados
¼   cup diced white onion
¼   cup chopped fresh cilantro
2   garlic cloves, peeled
1   jalapeño chile pepper, split open and seeded
    Grated zest and juice of 1 lime
1   teaspoon honey
1   teaspoon coarse salt
1   teaspoon freshly ground black pepper
    Tortilla chips, for serving

Preheat the oven to 450°F.

Remove the husks from the tomatillos. Rinse under warm water and wipe clean. Cover a baking sheet with foil. Cut the tomatillos in half and put them on the baking sheet. Drizzle with the olive oil and roast for 20 minutes, until they are tender. Remove from the oven and let cool.

Cut each avocado in half lengthwise. Remove the pit from the avocado and discard. Remove the avocado from the skin, and place the avocado flesh in the bowl of a food processor. Add the cooled tomatillos, onion, cilantro, garlic, jalapeño, lime zest and juice, honey, salt, and pepper to the bowl. Pulse for 1 to 2 minutes, until smooth and creamy. Adjust the salt and pepper if needed.

Serve immediately with your favorite tortilla chips.

avocado kopanisti

Kopanisti is a whipped feta dish that is frequently served at Mediterranean restaurants. The saltiness of the feta is a great complement to a creamy avocado. I use this as a dip with fresh pita and crudités, or sometimes I use it as a spread on a panini or sandwich. It adds an extra layer of flavor to any dish.

Prep Time: 10 minutes
Total Time: 10 minutes
Serves: 6 to 8

1 Hass avocado

6 ounces Greek feta cheese

1 roasted red bell pepper (about 4 ounces)

2 tablespoons extra-virgin olive oil

1 or 2 garlic cloves, peeled

1 teaspoon coarse salt
Freshly ground black pepper to taste

1 teaspoon red pepper flakes
Pita chips or assorted crudités, for serving

1 tablespoon minced fresh parsley, for garnish (optional)

Cut the avocado in half lengthwise. Remove the pit from the avocado and discard. Remove the avocado from the skin, and place the avocado flesh in a food processor bowl. Add the feta, red bell pepper, olive oil, garlic, and salt to the bowl. Pulse for 1 to 2 minutes, until smooth and creamy. Adjust the salt and pepper if needed. Add the red pepper flakes and mix through.

Serve immediately with pita chips or crudités, or refrigerate for up to 3 days. Just before serving, garnish with the parsley, if desired.

avocado-cilantro hummus

Guacamole, meet hummus. Hummus, meet guacamole. Basically it's a match made in heaven. This super and extra-creamy hummus will knock your socks off and make you wish that you had introduced guacamole and hummus much sooner.

Prep Time: 5 minutes
Total Time: 5 minutes
Serves: 6 to 8

1   Hass avocado

1   15-ounce can garbanzo
    beans, rinsed and drained

½   cup extra-virgin olive oil

⅓   cup chopped fresh cilantro

1   jalapeño chile pepper, seeded

1   tablespoon fresh lemon juice

4   teaspoons tahini

1   teaspoon Tabasco or Tapatío
    hot sauce

1   teaspoon coarse salt
    Pita chips or assorted
    crudités, for serving

Cut the avocado in half lengthwise. Remove the pit from the avocado and discard. Remove the avocado from the skin, and place the avocado flesh in a food processor bowl.

Add the garbanzo beans, olive oil, cilantro, jalapeño, lemon juice, tahini, hot sauce, and salt to the bowl. Process the ingredients for 20 to 30 seconds, until the mixture is smooth. Taste and adjust the salt if needed.

Serve immediately with pita chips or crudités, or refrigerate for up to 3 days.

avocado caesar dressing

Does the raw egg in Caesar dressing freak anyone else out? I was so scared of Caesar dressings for the longest time as a child and refused to eat them until I discovered that the fresh mayo could easily be replaced by avocado! Problem solved.

Prep Time: 5 minutes
Total Time: 5 minutes
Serves: 6 to 8
(makes about 1½ cups)

1   Hass avocado
⅓ cup extra-virgin olive oil, plus
      more if needed
¼ cup grated Parmesan cheese
2   tablespoons red wine vinegar
1   tablespoon fresh lemon juice
      1 or 2 garlic cloves, peeled
¾ teaspoon Worcestershire sauce
¼ teaspoon coarse salt
¼ teaspoon freshly ground black
      pepper

Cut the avocado in half lengthwise. Remove the pit from the avocado and discard. Remove the avocado from the skin, and place the avocado flesh in a food processor bowl.

Add the olive oil, Parmesan, vinegar, lemon juice, garlic cloves, Worcestershire, salt, and pepper. Pulse for 1 to 2 minutes, until smooth and creamy. Adjust the salt and pepper if needed.

Use immediately, or refrigerate for up to 3 days.

avocado-basil pesto

When my obsession with avocados began a few years ago, I basically put avocado in everything. And "everything" includes pesto. This pesto tastes like the typical basil-packed pesto that you're used to, but it also has a creamy texture that makes it the perfect sauce for chicken, fish, pasta, or any other dish that pesto complements!

Prep Time: 10 minutes
Cook Time: 3 minutes
Total Time: 13 minutes
Serves: 6 to 8
(about 1½ cups)

2 tablespoons pine nuts (or chopped walnuts)
1 Hass avocado
1 cup packed fresh basil leaves
¼ cup grated Parmesan cheese
2 garlic cloves, peeled
1 teaspoon coarse salt
¼ teaspoon freshly ground black pepper
¼ cup extra-virgin olive oil, plus more as needed

To toast the pine nuts, set a small skillet over medium-low heat. Add the pine nuts and gently shake the skillet frequently while cooking to ensure even browning. When the nuts are fragrant and golden brown, after 2 to 3 minutes, turn off the heat. Transfer the pine nuts to a small plate to cool.

Cut the avocado in half lengthwise. Remove the pit from the avocado and discard. Remove the avocado from the skin, and place the avocado flesh in a food processor bowl.

Add the pine nuts, basil, Parmesan, garlic, salt, and pepper to the bowl. Pulse the mixture for 1 to 2 minutes while streaming in the olive oil, until smooth and creamy. Scrape down the sides of the food processor bowl with a spatula as needed. Adjust the salt and pepper if needed.

Use immediately, or transfer the pesto to a small container with a tight-fitting lid and cover with olive oil to ensure the pesto does not brown. Refrigerate for up to 3 days.

avocado lime vinaigrette

This is my go-to vinaigrette! So many times I come home from cooking for my clients and I want to spend less than 20 minutes in my own kitchen. My solution more times than not involves this vinaigrette, some fresh greens from the farmers' market, and some grilled fish. The honey in this dressing gives the vinaigrette the perfect hint of sweetness and makes for a drool-inducing dressing.

Prep Time: 5 to 10 minutes
Total Time: 5 to 10 minutes
Serves: 6 to 8
(about 1 cup)

½ Hass avocado
½ cup extra-virgin olive oil, plus more if needed
¼ cup packed fresh cilantro
2 tablespoons pine nuts
   Juice of 1 lime
2 teaspoons red wine vinegar
2 teaspoons honey or agave nectar
1 teaspoon finely diced serrano chile pepper
   Coarse salt and freshly ground black pepper to taste

Remove the pit from the avocado half and discard. Remove the avocado from the skin, and place the avocado flesh in a food processor bowl.

Add the olive oil, cilantro, pine nuts, lime juice, vinegar, honey, and serrano pepper to the bowl. Pulse the mixture for 1 to 2 minutes, until smooth and creamy. If the vinaigrette is still too thick, stream in a bit more olive oil to thin it out. Season with the salt and pepper.

Store the vinaigrette in a small container in the refrigerator for up to 2 days.

did you know?

Avocados were first introduced to the U.S. in 1871, when Judge R. B. Ord planted three trees in Santa Barbara, California.

cumin avocado corn salsa

There's nothing quite like an appetizer that does double duty and can be used as part of the main dish too. Cumin Avocado Corn Salsa is a bright and cheerful way to greet your guests when you're having people over. They can snack on it with chips and you can use it to top some grilled meat or fish too.

Prep Time: 10 minutes
Total Time: 40 minutes
(includes chilling time)
Serves: 6 to 8
(about 3 cups)

3 ears of corn, husks and silks removed
1 Hass avocado
1 cup quartered cherry tomatoes
½ cup finely chopped red onion
   Juice of 1 lime
2 tablespoons finely chopped fresh chives
2 tablespoons finely chopped fresh cilantro
2 tablespoons finely chopped jalapeño chile pepper
½ teaspoon ground cumin
   Coarse salt and freshly ground black pepper to taste
   Tortilla chips, for serving

Cut the kernels off the cobs by laying each cob flat on a cutting board and using a sharp knife to remove the kernels. Transfer the kernels to a large bowl.

Cut the avocado in half lengthwise. Remove the pit from the avocado and discard. Remove the avocado from the skin, and cut the avocado into ½-inch pieces. Transfer to the bowl with the corn.

Add the cherry tomatoes, red onion, lime juice, chives, cilantro, jalapeño, and cumin to the bowl. Toss the ingredients together to combine, and season with salt and pepper. Refrigerate the salsa for 30 minutes before serving.

Taste and adjust salt and pepper as needed before serving. Serve with tortilla chips.

tropical pineapple salsa

Sometimes you just want to pretend that you're in the tropics. With a cocktail or two. And some tropical pineapple salsa, of course! The contrast in flavor from the pineapple and avocado makes for a match made in heaven. And the burst of color and spice from the red pepper will make this salsa a party in your mouth.

Prep Time: 10 minutes
Total Time: 40 minutes (including chilling time)
Serves: 6 to 8
(about 2 cups)

1 Hass avocado
1 cup diced fresh pineapple
    (¼-inch pieces)
¼ cup finely diced red onion
2 thinly sliced scallions, green
    parts only
2 tablespoons finely chopped
    red jalapeño chile pepper
1 tablespoon chopped fresh
    cilantro
1 tablespoon fresh lime juice
    Coarse salt and freshly
    ground black pepper to taste
    Tortilla chips, for serving

Cut the avocado in half lengthwise. Remove the pit from the avocado and discard. Remove the avocado from the skin, and cut the avocado into ¼-inch pieces. Transfer the avocado to a bowl.

Add the diced pineapple, red onion, scallions, jalapeño, cilantro, and lime juice. Toss to combine and season with salt and pepper.

Let the salsa chill for 30 minutes in the refrigerator before serving. Serve with tortilla chips.

avocado crema

Back in my days of being the pickiest eater on the planet, I would have looked at the word *crema* and had a small panic attack. Now, I can't get enough. Drizzle some of this avocado crema onto some nachos, quesadillas, or basically anything else, and you'll find that it enhances the flavor of that dish!

Prep Time: 5 minutes
Total Time: 5 minutes
Serves: 8 (about 1 cup)

1 Hass avocado
¼ cup sour cream
2 tablespoons chopped fresh cilantro
2 teaspoons fresh lime juice
2% milk, as needed
Coarse salt to taste

Cut the avocado in half lengthwise. Remove the pit from the avocado and discard. Remove the avocado from the skin, and place the avocado in a food processor bowl. Add the sour cream, cilantro, and lime juice and pulse for 1 minute, until smooth. Add about 1 tablespoon milk—just enough until the mixture thins out to the consistency of a ranch dressing. Add another tablespoon of milk if you need to thin it out even more. Season with salt as needed. Transfer the crema to a bowl and cover with plastic wrap until ready to use.

appetizers

I mean, who doesn't want to start a meal with avocado? I maintain my stance that the avocado is the world's best fruit and that it makes just about everybody happy. I love throwing a casual dinner party and wowing my guests with an avocado appetizer right off the bat.

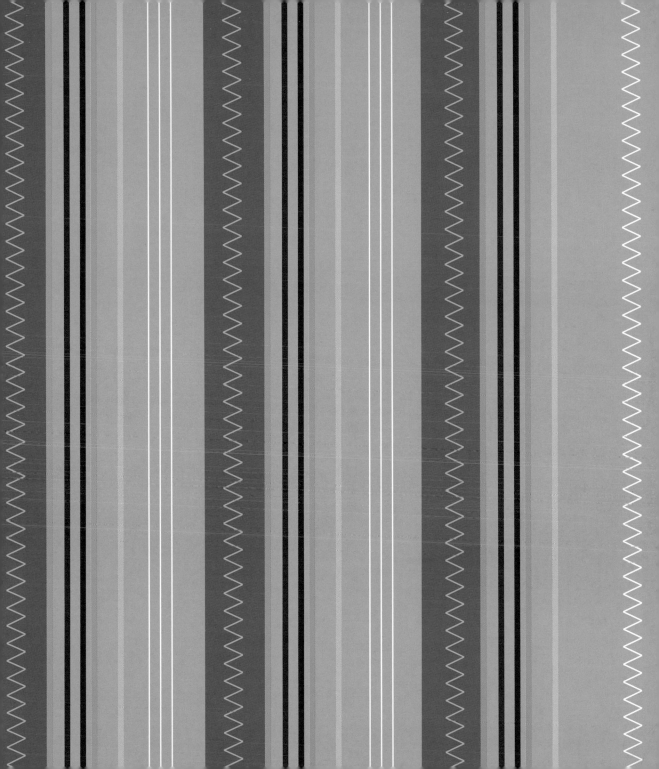

avocado-stuffed potato skins

Even though this recipe says it serves 8 to 10, be prepared to eat the entire thing by yourself. These little bites of potato filled with cheese, salty pancetta, and smashed avocado will totally rock your world. Serve them for a game day or a fun backyard bash and they will disappear off the table faster than you'll believe.

Prep Time: 10 minutes
Cook Time: 40 minutes
Total Time: 80 minutes
(including cooling time)
Serves: 8 to 10

12 baby yellow potatoes
 3 tablespoons extra-virgin olive oil
 4 ounces pancetta, diced
1½ cups shredded cheddar cheese
 2 tablespoons finely chopped red onion
 2 Hass avocados
    Juice of 1 lemon
 2 tablespoons finely chopped fresh chives
 ½ teaspoon coarse salt
 ½ teaspoon freshly ground black pepper

Preheat the oven to 400°F.

Drizzle the whole potatoes with the olive oil, making sure they are all evenly coated, and lay them on a parchment-lined baking sheet. Bake for 30 to 35 minutes or until the potatoes are fork-tender. Remove the potatoes from the oven and let them rest until they are cool enough to handle.

Cut the potatoes in half lengthwise so that you have 24 pieces. Carefully scoop out the middle portion of each halved potato so the remaining portion looks like a little potato cup. Set aside the scooped-out potato flesh for another use.

Put the cut potatoes back onto the baking sheet, cut side up.

Add the pancetta to a small skillet over medium-high heat. Let the pancetta start to crisp while occasionally stirring. Once the pancetta is golden brown, remove it from the skillet with a slotted spoon and transfer to a paper towel–lined plate to drain the excess fat.

Toss together the pancetta, cheese, and red onion in a small bowl. Evenly distribute the mixture in the potato skins on the baking sheet. Put the baking sheet back in the oven for 5 to 6 minutes, until the cheese has just melted.

While the cheese is melting, cut each avocado in half lengthwise. Remove the pit from the avocado and discard. Remove the avocado from the skin, and cut the avocado into small dice. Transfer to a medium bowl. Add the lemon juice, chives, salt, and pepper and mash together with a fork.

Once the cheese has melted in the potato skins, remove the baking sheet from the oven. Let the potatoes cool slightly, and then top with the guacamole mixture.

Serve immediately.

avocado bruschetta with balsamic drizzle

I'm a bruschetta girl through and through, but oftentimes
I get bummed out when the tomato topping falls off the
bread. Does this happen to anyone else, or am I clearly
challenged when it comes to eating bruschetta? Well, not
anymore, because these bruschetta, topped with smashed
avocado and a balsamic vinegar drizzle, are the perfect
starter for any meal and super easy to eat. If you can't find
the balsamic crème in your local market, reduce some
balsamic vinegar on the stovetop until syrupy and use that
instead.

Prep Time: 5 minutes
Cook Time: 5 minutes
Total Time: 10 minutes
Serves: 6 to 8

1 French baguette (about
   16 inches)
¼ cup extra-virgin olive oil
2 garlic cloves, halved
3 Hass avocados
¼ cup chopped fresh chives
10 basil leaves, thinly sliced
   Coarse salt and freshly
    ground black pepper to taste
   Balsamic crème, for drizzling
    (a balsamic glaze that can
    be found near the vinegar
    section in the market)

Preheat the oven to 450°F.

Slice the baguette into ½-inch-thick slices on the diagonal. Brush the top of
each piece of bread with olive oil using a pastry brush. Lay the pieces of bread
on a baking sheet and bake for 4 to 5 minutes, until the bread just begins to turn
golden brown. Remove the baking sheet from the oven, and while the pieces of
toast are still on the baking sheet, rub each piece of toast with the raw cut garlic.
Let the toasts cool.

Cut each avocado in half lengthwise. Remove the pit from the avocado and
discard. Remove the avocado from the skin, and place the avocado flesh in a
bowl.

Add the chives, basil, salt, and pepper. Mash with a fork until smooth and
creamy. Taste and add more salt and pepper if desired. Put 2 tablespoons of the
avocado mixture onto each piece of toast. Drizzle with a touch of the balsamic
crème before serving.

Serve immediately.

Note: Do not assemble these until you are ready to serve them, as the avocado
topping will make the bread soggy if it sits for too long.

classic cheese crisps

Cheese crisps were my life. They still are my life! Growing up in Tucson, Arizona, the rumored home of the cheese crisp, meant that I was introduced to these small baked tortillas topped with melted gooey cheese very early in my life. And that meant one thing: Cheese crisps were always the answer. Come home from tennis, have a cheese crisp. Bored at home on the weekend, have a cheese crisp. Parents not home for dinner, make you and your sibling some cheese crisps. These crazy-simple baked tortillas piled high with cheese and guacamole are basically the best things on earth.

Prep Time: 5 minutes
Cook Time: 10 minutes
Total Time: 15 minutes
Serves: 2

4   small flour tortillas
4   teaspoons (½ stick) butter, at
      room temperature
1   cup shredded cheese (cheddar,
      queso quesadilla, Oaxaca)
¼   cup thinly sliced scallions
1   batch Bacon-Cotija Guacamole
      (page 55)

Preheat the oven to 350°F.

Lay the tortillas on a baking sheet. Spread 1 teaspoon of the butter on each tortilla. Put the baking sheet into the oven and toast for 5 to 7 minutes, until golden brown. Remove the baking sheet from the oven.

Sprinkle ¼ cup of the cheese on top of each tortilla and put the baking sheet back into the oven for 3 to 4 minutes, until the cheese has completely melted.

Sprinkle the cheese crisps with the scallions, top with the guacamole, and serve immediately.

tostones with chunky avocado

I was never that into plantains until a recent trip to Belize. Our gracious hosts cooked us plantains for breakfast, lunch, and dinner, and I quickly fell in love with this versatile item. When buying plantains, you want to look for a yellow plantain with a few black marks on its skin. If it's too dark and almost all black, it's too ripe to fry. If it's green, then it's not ripe enough. A yellow-black plantain is just about perfect.

Prep Time: 10 minutes
Cook Time: 10 minutes
Total Time: 20 minutes
Serves: 6 to 8

2　ripe yellow to yellow-black plantains
½　cup vegetable oil
　　Coarse salt to taste
2　Hass avocados
1　ripe mango
　　Juice of 1 lemon
　　Freshly ground black pepper to taste
¼　cup finely diced red onion

Peel each plantain. Cut each plantain into 6 to 8 pieces.

Heat the oil in a large heavy skillet over medium heat until shimmering. Add 6 pieces of plantain at a time and cook, turning every 30 seconds, until just golden brown. Remove the plantains from the oil with a pair of tongs and repeat this process for the remaining plantains.

Using a tortilla press, carefully press down on each piece of semi-cooked plantain until you have a 2- to 3-inch flat disk. If you don't have a tortilla press, simply press down on the semi-cooked plantain with a small flat bottomed plate until the plantain is a 2- to 3-inch flat disk. Fry these disks in the oil for about 45 seconds on each side, until a deeper golden color. Transfer the disks to a paper towel to drain; sprinkle with salt. Repeat with remaining plantains.

Cut each avocado in half lengthwise. Remove the pit from the avocado and discard. Remove the avocado from the skin, cut into ½-inch dice, and place in a bowl. Using a vegetable peeler, remove the skin of the mango. Using a sharp knife, slice the wide flat part of the fruit off the pit. Repeat this process for the other side of the mango. Transfer the 2 mango slices to a cutting board and cut into ½-inch pieces. Add the mango to the bowl with the avocado.

Add the lemon juice and toss to combine. Season with salt and pepper. Top each of the fried plantains with equal portions of the avocado mixture. Top each tostone with a sprinkle of the red onion, and serve immediately.

parmesan-panko avocado fries

Fries don't always have to be made out of potatoes. Panko- and Parmesan-crusted avocado slices clearly make for an irresistible snack and make fries even more fun. Throw in some chipotle ranch dressing and you've got one of the best snacks ever. Times a million.

Prep Time: 10 minutes
Cook Time: 10 minutes
Total Time: 20 minutes
Serves: 4

Grapeseed oil, for frying
¼ cup all-purpose flour
½ teaspoon sweet paprika
½ teaspoon coarse salt, plus
    more to taste
1 large egg
1 tablespoon 1% milk
1 cup panko bread crumbs
½ cup grated Parmesan cheese
2 Hass avocados
Chipotle ranch dressing, for
    serving

In a large deep skillet, heat about 1 inch of grapeseed oil over medium-high heat.

Meanwhile, prepare the breading station. In one medium bowl, combine the flour, paprika, and salt, and stir to combine. In another bowl, combine the egg and milk, and whisk together. In another bowl, combine the panko and Parmesan.

Cut each avocado in half lengthwise. Remove the pit from the avocado and discard. Remove the avocado from the skin, and cut each half into 3 wedges, making a total of 12 pieces.

One by one, dip the avocado in the flour mixture and dust off any excess flour. Next, dip the avocado in the egg mixture. Finally, dip the avocado into the panko-Parmesan mixture. Lay the breaded avocado on a baking sheet and repeat this process for the remaining avocado wedges.

Once the oil begins to shimmer, about 350°F on a thermometer, fry a few avocado slices at a time for 45 to 60 seconds total, flipping the fries after about 20 seconds, until they are golden brown. Transfer the fries with a slotted spoon to a paper towel–lined plate. Sprinkle with salt. Repeat the frying process for the remaining avocado, and then serve immediately with chipotle ranch dressing for dipping.

did you know?

The Hass is the most common avocado in the United States & is the only avocado grown year-round.

bacon-wrapped cheesy avocados

What's the one ingredient that is better than bacon?
Avocados, of course! So clearly these bacon-wrapped
avocados stuffed with a touch of goat cheese are going
to rock your world. The bacon is nice and crispy wrapped
around a bit of tangy goat cheese and then perched on top
of a creamy avocado slice. Does it get any better?

Prep Time: 5 minutes
Cook Time: 15 to 20 minutes
Total Time: 20 to 25 minutes
Serves: 4

2 Hass avocados
4 strips bacon
8 teaspoons goat cheese
   Freshly ground black pepper
      to taste

Preheat the oven to 400°F.

Cut each avocado in half lengthwise. Remove the pit from the avocado and
discard. Remove the avocado from the skin, and cut each half into 2 pieces,
making a total of 8 pieces.

Lay the bacon on a cutting board. Cut the bacon in half lengthwise so you
have 8 long strips.

Put 1 teaspoon of the goat cheese in the cavity of each quartered avocado.
Wrap 1 piece of bacon around each goat cheese–stuffed quartered avocado
and secure with a toothpick so the ends don't come apart.

Put the bacon-wrapped avocados on a baking sheet and transfer to the oven
for 15 to 20 minutes, until the bacon is crispy. Let the bacon-wrapped cheesy
avocados rest for 5 minutes. Sprinkle a touch of freshly ground black pepper
over each piece before serving.

grilled avocado & salsa

Have you ever tried to grill an avocado? It's super easy and fun. The hint of smoke from the grill makes this the perfect start to a meal. Especially when you load up the avocado with some pico de gallo.

Prep Time: 5 minutes
Cook Time: 5 minutes
Total Time: 10 minutes
Serves: 2

1 Hass avocado
1 teaspoon extra-virgin olive oil
1 teaspoon fresh lime juice
  Coarse salt and freshly
    ground black pepper to taste
¼ cup pico de gallo

Prepare a gas or charcoal grill.

Cut the avocado in half lengthwise. Remove the pit from the avocado and discard, but leave the peel on. Brush the exposed part of the avocado with the olive oil and lime juice.

Lay the avocado, flesh side down, on the grill and let cook for 2 minutes. Rotate the avocado 90 degrees and continue to grill for 2 to 3 minutes more, until there are grill marks. Sprinkle with salt and pepper and spoon 2 tablespoons of pico de gallo into each of the avocado cavities.

Serve immediately.

chorizo gravy guacamole loaded nachos

What happens when two of your best friends make chorizo gravy biscuits for breakfast and there is leftover chorizo gravy? The Chorizo Gravy Guacamole Loaded Nachos, of course! Matt and Adam, the geniuses behind the photography and food styling in this book, and two of my best friends, made the most decadent chorizo gravy–laced biscuits one day while we were vacationing in Palm Springs. My fiancé (at the time) and I, being the nacho fanatics we are, decided that the extra gravy needn't be tossed but instead should be incorporated into that day's lunch. Thus Chorizo Gravy Guacamole Loaded Nachos were born. And trust me, you'll never want to have any other nachos ever again. If queso quesadilla isn't readily available, substitute shredded Monterey Jack.

Prep Time: 15 minutes
Cook Time: 10 minutes
Total Time: 25 minutes
Serves: 6 to 8

1   canned chipotle chile pepper in adobo sauce
3   ounces Mexican pork chorizo
1   tablespoon butter
1   tablespoon all-purpose flour
1   cup 1% milk, warmed
10 ounces tortilla chips
10 ounces shredded queso quesadilla (found in the Hispanic section of the market)
8   ounces shredded Mexican-style cheese
1   cup pico de gallo
1   batch Chipotle Guacamole (page 52)
¼   cup chopped pickled jalapeño chile peppers
2   tablespoons chopped fresh chives
2   tablespoons thinly sliced scallions

Finely mince the chipotle pepper and transfer it to a medium saucepan with the chorizo over medium-high heat. Cook the chorizo, stirring occasionally and breaking up the meat, until fully cooked and browned, about 5 minutes. Add the butter and stir until melted. Add the flour and stir to combine. Let the flour cook for 1 minute, and then whisk in the milk. Bring the mixture to a boil while stirring. Once the gravy thickens, remove from the heat and set aside.

Preheat the oven to 350°F.

Lay the tortilla chips on a baking sheet in a single layer. (For easy cleanup, line the baking sheet with parchment paper.) Drizzle on the chorizo gravy, followed by the queso quesadilla and Mexican-style cheese. Bake for 5 minutes, until the cheese is fully melted.

Sprinkle the nachos with pico de gallo, guacamole, pickled jalapeños, chives, and scallions. Serve immediately.

wraps & sandwiches

Sitting down to a leisurely lunch might just be one of my favorite activities. I love the idea of actually enjoying your lunch and being able to socialize with your friends and coworkers rather than just eating quickly at your desk. These sandwich and lunch-type dishes are perfect for doing just that. They will leave you satisfied and happy, especially because each of them is stuffed with avocados!

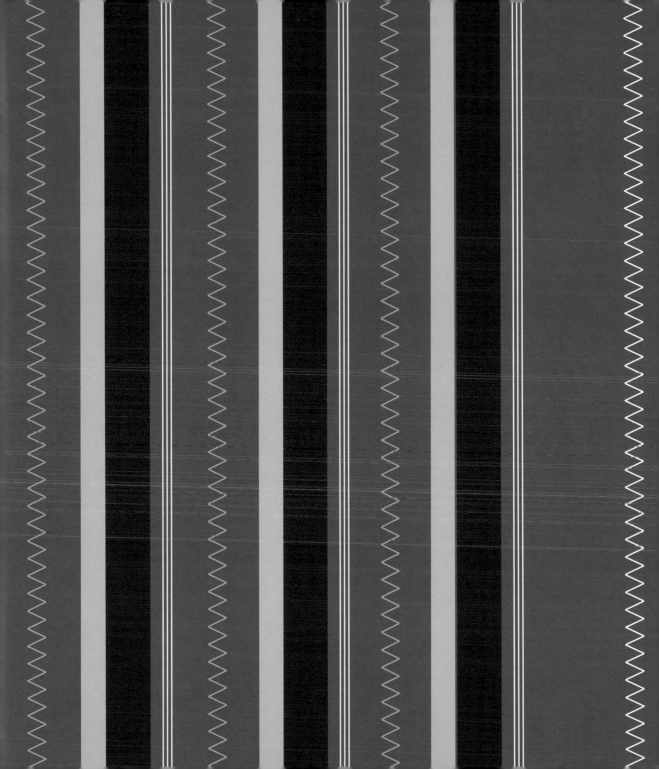

hawaiian pulled pork & avocado sandwich

Pineapple, pork, and homemade barbecue sauce, all cooked together for multiple hours until the meat is literally falling apart and then served on top of a toasted bun, is my definition of comfort food. I make this with chunks of pineapple because I like the burst of sweetness when I bite into a piece, but you could easily use crushed pineapple if that's more your style. Just be sure to discard the excess juice so it doesn't make your pork too sweet.

Prep Time: 10 minutes
Cook Time: 8 hours
Total Time: 8 hours and 10 minutes
Serves: 6

2   pounds pork shoulder, excess fat trimmed

1   8-ounce can cubed pineapple, drained

1   large yellow onion, finely chopped

¼   cup ketchup

½   cup apple cider vinegar

¼   cup packed light brown sugar

2   tablespoons tomato paste

2   tablespoons sweet paprika

2   tablespoons Worcestershire sauce

2   teaspoons red pepper flakes

1   teaspoon dried mustard

1   teaspoon coarse salt

1   teaspoon freshly ground black pepper

2   Hass avocados

6   ciabatta rolls, sliced (or your favorite hamburger bun)

4   teaspoons butter

Cut the pork into 2-inch pieces and place in a 6½ quart slow cooker. Add the diced pineapple, onion, ketchup, vinegar, brown-sugar, tomato paste, sweet paprika, Worcestershire sauce, red pepper flakes, dried mustard, salt, and pepper. Set the slow cooker on the low heat setting and cook for 8 hours, until the pork is fork-tender and falling apart. While the meat is still in the slow cooker, use two forks to shred the pork.

Cut the avocados in half lengthwise. Remove the pit from the avocado and discard. Remove the avocado from the skin, and cut it into thin slices. Set aside.

Preheat the oven to broil.

Spread both sides of the ciabatta rolls with butter and toast under the broiler for a few minutes, until just toasted and golden brown.

Using a pair of tongs, grab about ½ cup of the pork mixture, let most of the liquid drain off, and place it on the bottom of a ciabatta roll. Top with a few slices of avocado and the remaining half of the ciabatta roll. Repeat this process for the remaining ciabatta rolls. Serve immediately.

avocado cheesesteak

Thin slices of steak along with thin slices of avocado smothered with provolone cheese on a buttered and toasted roll? I'll take two, please. It doesn't get much better than this California-influenced avocado cheesesteak.

Prep Time: 10 minutes
Cook Time: 30 minutes
Total Time: 40 minutes
Serves: 2

1   pound top round steak
1   large yellow onion
6   tablespoons butter
    Coarse salt to taste
4   slices provolone cheese
2   8-inch hoagie rolls, sliced
1   Hass avocado
    Freshly ground black pepper
      to taste

Place the top round steak in the freezer. (Keeping the steak in the freezer for 20 minutes while you caramelize the onions will make the steak much easier to cut.)

Cut the onion in half and remove the skin. Cut the onion into ¼-inch slices. Heat 2 tablespoons of the butter in a large skillet over medium-high heat. Add the onion and season with salt. Cook the onions, stirring occasionally, for a few minutes, until they begin to turn golden brown. Reduce the heat to medium-low and let the onions cook for 20 minutes longer, stirring every few minutes to ensure they don't burn. Once the onions are a dark golden color, remove them from the skillet and set aside.

Remove the top round steak from the freezer and transfer the steak to a cutting board. Using a very sharp knife, cut the steak against the grain into super-thin slices. You want the steak to be as thin as possible, almost transparent. Add 2 tablespoons of the butter to the same skillet over medium-high heat. Add the steak to the butter and, using two forks, pull the meat apart so it cooks evenly. Cook the steak for 2 to 3 minutes, until cooked through. Add the provolone on top of the steak, reduce the heat to low, and cover the skillet with its lid. Let the cheese melt for 2 to 3 minutes and then remove the lid.

Preheat the oven to broil.

Spread the remaining 2 tablespoons of butter on the inside of the hoagie rolls. Toast the bread under the broiler for a few minutes, until just lightly golden. Divide the meat mixture evenly among the hoagie rolls.

Cut the avocado in half lengthwise. Remove the pit from the avocado and discard. Remove the avocado from the skin, and cut it into thin slices.

Top the meat with the thinly sliced avocado and season with salt and pepper. Serve immediately.

crab & avocado quesadilla

Quesadillas were one of the few things I used to make for myself as a kid. I would pile high the cheese and nuke it in the microwave until the cheese was just melted. These days, I'm still a quesadilla kinda girl, but I've upped the ante and started stuffing these with crab and Monterey Jack cheese. They are great when you're in a hurry but still want a decadent and delicious dinner.

Prep Time: 10 minutes
Cook Time: 10 minutes
Total Time: 20 minutes
Serves: 2 to 4

1½ cups grated Monterey Jack cheese

4 scallions

½ cup finely diced red bell pepper

¼ cup fresh corn kernels

¼ cup finely diced red onion

2 tablespoons chopped pickled jalapeño chile peppers

1 Hass avocado

½ lime

4 8-inch flour tortillas

8 ounces lump crabmeat, picked over for shells

1 batch Tomatillo-Avocado Salsa (page 66)

Put the grated cheese in a large bowl. Slice the scallions into thin rings and place them in the bowl with the cheese. Add the red pepper, corn, red onion, and pickled jalapeños to the cheese and toss to combine.

Cut the avocado in half lengthwise. Remove the pit from the avocado and discard. Remove the avocado from the skin, and cut each half of the avocado into 8 thin strips. Squeeze a little lime juice on top of the avocado strips.

Heat a large heavy skillet over medium heat. Put one of the tortillas into the skillet and sprinkle with half of the cheese mixture, half of the crabmeat, and half of the thinly sliced avocado. Once the cheese begins to melt, add another tortilla on top. Using two spatulas, one on the bottom of the quesadilla and one to hold the top in place, flip the quesadilla to toast the other side. Once the cheese has fully melted and the tortilla is slightly crisp, remove the quesadilla from the skillet and repeat this process with the remaining ingredients.

Cut each quesadilla into 6 wedges and serve immediately with the dip.

open-faced avocado croque monsieur

I often revert back to my childhood eating habits when I'm feeling a little homesick, and nothing quite reminds me of home like a classic grilled cheese sandwich, made by my dad of course! Over the years, I've jazzed up my go-to childhood meal by adding salty prosciutto, thinly sliced avocado, and a creamy béchamel sauce that gets toasted under the broiler. This is sure to please any grilled cheese addict.

Prep Time: 10 minutes
Cook Time: 15 minutes
Total Time: 25 minutes
Serves: 4

3 tablespoons butter
1 tablespoon all-purpose flour
1 cup 1% milk
1¼ cups grated Gruyère cheese
¼ teaspoon ground mustard
⅛ teaspoon ground nutmeg
   Coarse salt and freshly
      ground black pepper to taste
1 Hass avocado
4 ¾-inch-thick slices French
      bread
8 thin slices prosciutto

Preheat the oven to 400°F.

Add 1 tablespoon of the butter to a medium skillet over medium heat. Once the butter has melted, add the flour and whisk together until golden. Stream in the milk and whisk until the mixture starts to thicken. Add ¼ cup of the grated Gruyère, the ground mustard, and ground nutmeg. Whisk the mixture until the cheese is melted. Season with salt and pepper and set aside.

Cut the avocado in half lengthwise. Remove the pit from the avocado and discard. Remove the avocado from the skin and thinly slice the avocado. Set aside.

Spread the remaining 2 tablespoons butter on the 4 pieces of bread and place the bread, butter side up, on a parchment-lined baking sheet. Transfer the baking sheet to the oven and toast for about 5 minutes, until golden brown. Remove the baking sheet from the oven and flip the bread over.

Preheat the oven to broil.

Top the bread with equal amounts of prosciutto, followed by the thinly sliced avocado and the remaining 1 cup Gruyère. Spoon a few tablespoons of the Gruyère sauce over the open-faced sandwiches and broil until the top is golden brown, 3 to 4 minutes.

Sprinkle with salt and pepper. Serve immediately.

did you know?

Rudolph Hass, a postman, patented the Hass avocado tree in 1935.

turkey malibu panini

How much do we all love a good panino? There's nothing quite like that toasted bread, melted cheese, and some protein to satisfy your hunger. This sandwich is extra delicious because of the kopanisti spread!

Prep Time: 5 minutes
Cook Time: 5 minutes
Total Time: 10 minutes
Serves: 2

4   slices French bread
½   batch Avocado Kopanisti
      (page 67)
4   medium-thick slices roasted
      turkey breast
4   slices prosciutto
1   Hass avocado
4   slices pepper Jack cheese
1   cup spinach leaves
2   tablespoons chopped sun-
      dried tomatoes
2   tablespoons extra-virgin olive
      oil

Preheat a panini press to a medium-high heat setting.

Arrange the bread on a cutting board. Spread a thin layer of the kopanisti onto 2 pieces of the bread. Add 2 pieces of turkey on top of the kopanisti, followed by 2 slices of prosciutto.

Cut the avocado in half lengthwise. Remove the pit from the avocado and discard. Remove the avocado from the skin, and cut it into thin slices.

Arrange the slices evenly on the 2 panini, along with the cheese, spinach, and sun-dried tomatoes. Top the panini with the remaining bread. Brush the top of the panini with olive oil and place them in the panini press for 4 to 5 minutes, until the bread is golden brown. Slice in half and serve immediately.

cheese-stuffed pupusas with tomatillo-avocado salsa

Every Sunday I drag myself out of bed so that I am one of the first people at my local farmers' market. This is for two reasons. First, I like to be the first one there to say hi to all my farmers and hear about what they brought this week. And second, I've got to get in line to get my breakfast. Behold, the pupusa. Made from a masa-based dough and stuffed with cheese and served with a spicy salsa, it's one of the best things on earth. While I still order one every Sunday at the market, I've had to start creating them at home too, to satisfy my midweek cravings.

Prep Time: 25 minutes
Cook Time: 30 t0 40 minutes
Total Time: 55 to 65 minutes
Serves: 5

2   cups masa harina
    1¾ to 2 cups warm water
1   teaspoon coarse salt
2   tablespoons cold water
¼   cup shredded Monterey Jack
    cheese
2   tablespoons extra-virgin olive
    oil
    Tomatillo-Avocado Salsa
    (page 66), for serving

In a large bowl, combine the masa harina, 1¾ cups of the warm water, and the salt and stir together until smooth. Using the palms of your hands, knead the dough together until it becomes one mass. You want the dough to be a similar consistency to Play-Doh. If it feels too dry, add the remaining ¼ cup warm water and knead again. Let the dough rest for 20 minutes.

Add the 2 tablespoons cold water to the rested dough and knead the dough for 2 minutes, until the water is fully incorporated.

Divide the dough into 10 equal pieces, about 2 ounces each, and roll into balls the size of golf balls.

Hold one of the balls of dough in the palm of your hand. Gently press your free thumb into the center of the ball to form an indentation. Then start to flatten the dough to form a larger disk so it looks like a small bowl. To the center of the disk, add 2 teaspoons of the cheese. Bring the edges of the disk over the cheese and squeeze together to form a ball shape of dough so the cheese is secured inside. Gently work the ball of dough into a flat disk about 3 inches in diameter. Brush the disk with olive oil, place on a plate, and cover with a clean, damp kitchen towel. Repeat this process for the remaining pupusas.

Heat a large skillet over medium-high heat. Lay 2 pupusas in the skillet at a time and cook for 3 to 4 minutes on each side, until the outsides are golden brown and the dough has slightly puffed.

Serve immediately with the salsa.

salads

Bright, beautiful, avocado-loaded salads are my life. Not to mention incredibly healthy! This collection of salads is going to make you swoon. Some are gorgeous knife-and-fork salads piled high with winter citrus, some are colorful summer salads that are perfect for any backyard summer bash, and some are easy weeknight salads that you'll want to start incorporating into your everyday life!

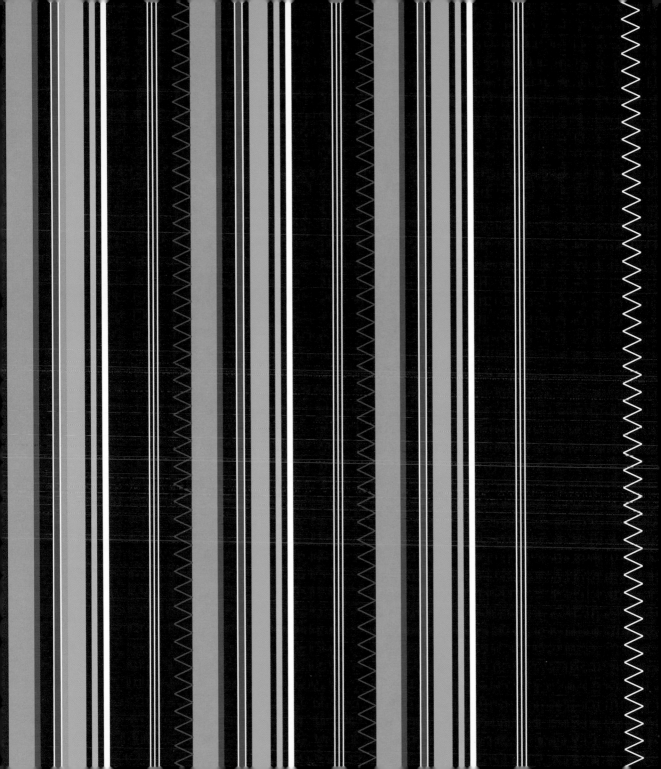

tropical avocado salad

There are a few reasons I'm a self-proclaimed salad freak. One, they are healthy. Two, they are fairly quick to make. And three, they are gorgeous! This one in particular. The bright color of the mango makes this salad a total looker. Don't worry, though—it tastes just as good as it looks, and you'll be left licking your lips for more.

Prep Time: 15 minutes
Total Time: 15 minutes
Serves: 4 to 6

2   Hass avocados
1   ripe mango
3   cups arugula
½   English cucumber, cut into half-moons
¼   red onion, thinly sliced
1   jalapeño chile pepper, seeded and sliced
2   tablespoons fresh orange juice
2   tablespoons champagne vinegar
⅓   cup avocado oil (extra-virgin olive oil may be substituted)
1   teaspoon coarse salt
½   teaspoon freshly ground black pepper

Cut each avocado in half lengthwise. Remove the pit from the avocado and discard. Remove the avocado from the skin, and cut it into medium dice. Set aside.

Using a vegetable peeler, remove the skin of the mango. Using a sharp knife, slice the wide flat part of the fruit off the pit. Repeat this process for the other side of the mango. Transfer the 2 mango slices to a cutting board and cut into ½-inch pieces.

In a large bowl, combine the arugula, mango, cucumber, red onion, and jalapeño and toss gently to combine. Add the diced avocado. Set aside. In a small bowl, combine the orange juice and vinegar. Slowly stream in the avocado oil while whisking together to form the dressing. Season with the salt and pepper.

Drizzle half of the dressing over the salad and toss. Taste and add more dressing if needed, being careful not to overdress it. Serve immediately.

grilled romaine & avocado salad

If you can grill chicken, steak, and fish, why can't you grill a salad? Well, good news guys, you can! This fork-and-knife salad is a winner. Slightly charred and smoky romaine lettuce, avocado, and red onion get paired with a Dijon vinaigrette that will have you begging for more.

Prep Time: 10 minutes
Cook Time: 12 minutes
Total Time: 22 minutes
Serves: 4

2   heads romaine lettuce
1   Hass avocado
½   red onion
¼   cup plus 2 teaspoons extra-
    virgin olive oil
3   teaspoons fresh lemon juice
1   tablespoon minced shallot
1   teaspoon Dijon mustard
½   teaspoon honey
    Coarse salt and freshly
    ground black pepper to taste
    Shaved Parmesan cheese, for
    garnish

Prepare a gas or charcoal grill.

Remove the most outer leaves of the romaine lettuce. Cut the remaining romaine lettuce in half lengthwise, leaving the root of the lettuce intact, and set aside.

Cut the avocado in half lengthwise. Remove the pit from the avocado and discard.

Cut the red onion into circles and remove the outermost layer.

Brush the romaine lettuce, avocado, and red onion with 2 teaspoons of the olive oil.

Transfer the romaine lettuce, cut side down, to the grill and cook for 4 minutes. Remove once the lettuce is slightly charred and transfer to a serving platter.

Transfer the avocado, flesh side down, to the grill and let cook for 2 minutes. Rotate the avocado 90 degrees and continue to grill for 2 minutes more. Remove the avocado halves from the grill and carefully remove the skin. Slice the avocado into thin strips and add it on top of the grilled romaine.

Transfer the red onion circles onto the grill and cook for about 2 minutes on each side, until slightly charred. Remove the red onion circles from the grill and cut in half to form half circles. Sprinkle the red onion over the romaine and avocado on the serving platter.

In a small bowl whisk together the remaining ¼ cup olive oil, lemon juice, shallot, Dijon mustard, and honey. Season with salt and pepper as needed.

Drizzle the vinaigrette over the salad. Top with shaved Parmesan and serve immediately.

avocado, burrata, & heirloom tomato caprese

Have you ever had burrata cheese? If not, you need it in your life immediately. And if you have had the pleasure of tasting this cheese, you know it's not even fair to compare it to other cheeses because it wins. Hands down. Every single time. This fancy Caprese salad uses gorgeous and colorful heirloom tomatoes, freshly made burrata cheese, and perfect slices of bright green avocado. It makes something that is already amazing, the regular Caprese, even better. If balsamic crème isn't available, reduce some balsamic vinegar until syrupy and use that instead.

Prep Time: 10 minutes
Total Time: 10 minutes
Serves: 6 to 8

2   Hass avocados
2   pounds colorful heirloom tomatoes
8   ounces burrata cheese
10 fresh basil leaves
4   teaspoons extra-virgin olive oil
4   teaspoons balsamic crème (a balsamic glaze that can be found near the vinegar section in your local market)
1   teaspoon dried oregano
    Coarse salt and freshly ground black pepper to taste

Cut each avocado in half lengthwise. Remove the pit from the avocado and discard. Remove the avocado from the skin, and slice it into thin slices.

Cut the tomatoes into thick slices, about ½ inch-thick. Arrange the tomatoes on a large platter. Top each tomato with a slice of avocado, followed by a spoonful of burrata cheese.

Cut the basil leaves into a chiffonade and sprinkle over the top of the burrata. Drizzle the olive oil and balsamic crème over the platter. Sprinkle the dried oregano, salt, and pepper on top and serve immediately.

bacon, avocado, & corn salad

By now you've probably realized that I have an obsession with avocado and bacon. They just seem to be a match made in heaven. This bright springtime and summertime salad will make a gorgeous addition to any table, and you'll have everyone from kids to adults gobbling up this delectable side.

Prep Time: 10 minutes
Cook Time: 15 minutes
Total Time: 25 minutes
Serves: 6 to 8

5   strips thick-cut bacon
4   ears corn, husks and silks
      removed
2   ounces cotija cheese (feta
      cheese may be substituted)
2   tablespoons chopped fresh
      cilantro
      Juice of 1 lime
1   Hass avocado
      Coarse salt and freshly
        ground black pepper to taste

Place a heavy skillet over medium heat. Arrange the bacon strips in the skillet and cook on both sides until the bacon is crisp, 5 to 6 minutes. Transfer to a paper towel–lined plate to dry. Remove all but 1 tablespoon of the bacon fat from the skillet.

Cut the kernels off each cob by laying the cob flat on a cutting board and using a sharp knife to remove the kernels. Discard the cobs and transfer the kernels to the skillet with the bacon fat. Cook the corn over medium-high heat until it is just slightly golden brown, about 5 minutes. Turn off the heat, crumble in the cotija cheese, and add the cilantro and lime juice. Let the mixture cool to room temperature. Roughly crumble the bacon into the corn mixture and toss to combine.

Cut the avocado in half lengthwise. Remove the pit from the avocado and discard. Remove the avocado from the skin, and cut the avocado into ½-inch pieces. Transfer the avocado to the skillet and toss.

Taste and season with salt and pepper before serving. Serve immediately at room temperature, or refrigerate for later. Bring to room temperature before serving.

mexican chopped salad

Loaded salads are my best friend in the summer months. I love cleaning out my fridge and pantry, throwing everything into a salad, and whipping up a fun dressing to pull it all together. This loaded salad happens to be one of my favorites, and it's always the perfect salad to serve to a big group of friends at a weekend picnic.

Prep Time: 15 minutes
Cook Time: 5 minutes
Total Time: 20 minutes
Serves: 6 to 8

2   Hass avocados
4   ears corn, husks and silks removed
1   tablespoon butter
3   scallions, thinly sliced
1   15-ounce can black beans, rinsed and drained
1   red bell pepper, diced
2   heads romaine lettuce, outer leaves discarded and chopped
1   cup packed fresh cilantro stems and leaves
½   cup avocado oil (extra-virgin olive oil may be substituted)
¼   cup fresh lime juice
2   teaspoons honey or agave nectar
½   teaspoon coarse salt
½   teaspoon freshly ground black pepper
5   ounces cotija cheese, crumbled (feta cheese may be substituted)

Cut each avocado in half lengthwise. Remove the pit from the avocado and discard. Remove the avocado from the skin, and cut it into medium dice. Set aside.

Cut the kernels off each cob by laying the cob flat on a cutting board and using a sharp knife to remove the kernels. Discard the cobs.

In a medium skillet, heat the butter over medium-high heat. Add the corn and cook, stirring occasionally, until the corn is slightly softened, about 3 minutes.

Add the scallions and stir to combine. Remove the skillet from the heat and let cool. Transfer the vegetables to a large bowl.

Add the diced avocado, black beans, red bell pepper, and romaine lettuce to the corn mixture and set aside.

Add the cilantro, avocado oil, lime juice, honey, salt, and pepper to a food processor or blender. Pulse for 2 to 3 minutes, until the mixture is bright green and smooth.

Dress the salad with half of the dressing and half of the cheese. Toss the salad, then taste and add more dressing if desired. Top with the remaining cotija cheese and serve immediately.

cucumber salad

Cucumber salads were my life as a kid! My mom would make one for dinner every night and I would always try to sneak a few bites before dinner because it was just so good! It's fresh and easy and makes for a perfect side salad with almost any dinner.

Prep Time: 10 minutes
Total Time: 10 minutes
Serves: 6

2 tablespoons extra-virgin olive oil
2 tablespoons balsamic vinegar
1 garlic clove, minced
1 English cucumber
2 Hass avocados
2 large tomatoes
   Coarse salt and freshly ground black pepper to taste

In a small bowl, whisk together the olive oil and balsamic vinegar. Add the garlic to the olive oil mixture. Set aside.

Peel the cucumber and trim the ends. Slice the cucumber in half lengthwise and then cut each half into ½-inch half-moons. Transfer the cucumbers to a salad bowl.

Cut each avocado in half lengthwise. Remove the pit from the avocado and discard. Remove the avocado from the skin, and cut the avocado into ½-inch pieces. Transfer the avocado to the salad bowl.

Cut the tomatoes into medium-thick wedges and add to the salad bowl.

Toss the cucumbers, avocado, and tomatoes with the dressing and season with salt and pepper as needed before serving.

avocado-broccoli slaw

Sometimes you've gotta skip the mayo and replace it with avocado. I mean, who wouldn't want a slaw smothered with a smooth avocado dressing? It's basically the perfect side dish to any barbecued meal and really helps take the heat off, if your mouth is on fire from a spicy piece of meat.

Prep Time: 10 minutes
Total Time: 10 minutes
Serves: 6 to 8

12 ounces packaged broccoli slaw
1   Hass avocado
½   cup extra-virgin olive oil
¼   cup packed fresh cilantro
2   tablespoons apple cider vinegar
2   tablespoons fresh lime juice
    Coarse salt and freshly ground black pepper to taste
1   bunch scallions

Put the broccoli slaw in a large bowl.

Cut the avocado in half lengthwise. Remove the pit from the avocado and discard. Remove the avocado from the skin, and place the avocado flesh in a food processor bowl.

Add the olive oil, cilantro, vinegar, and lime juice to the food processor and pulse for 1 to 2 minutes until smooth. Transfer the avocado mixture to the bowl with the broccoli slaw and toss to combine. Taste the slaw and season with salt and pepper as needed.

Thinly slice the scallions on a bias. Top the broccoli slaw with the scallions and serve immediately.

did you know?

One tree can produce between 150 and 500 avocados per year.

winter citrus & avocado salad

Knife-and-fork salads need to be more popular. So I'm bringing this offering to the table. Colorful layers of pale green lettuce, pink and orange citrus, and deeper green avocado make this salad the perfect way to brighten up a table during the winter months.

Prep Time: 10 minutes
Total Time: 10 minutes
Serves: 6

6 large Boston lettuce leaves
1 pink grapefruit
1 naval orange
1 tangerine
1 Hass avocado
¼ cup chopped fresh chives
1 teaspoon extra-virgin olive oil
½ teaspoon agave nectar
   Coarse salt and freshly
      ground black pepper to taste

Spread out the pieces of lettuce on a large serving platter.

Cut the top and bottom off the grapefruit. Stand the grapefruit on its bottom and carefully cut away the skin to reveal the pith-free flesh of the fruit. Turn the grapefruit back on its side and cut the citrus into six ¼- to ⅓-inch-thick slices. If there are any visible seeds once the citrus has been sliced, carefully remove those by poking them out with a small knife. Arrange 1 slice of the grapefruit on each Boston lettuce leaf. Repeat this process for the orange and tangerine.

Cut the avocado in half lengthwise. Remove the pit from the avocado and discard. Remove the avocado from the skin, and cut each half of the avocado into 6 strips. Add 2 strips on top of each citrus pile.

Sprinkle the chives on top of each Boston lettuce cup. Drizzle with the olive oil and agave nectar. Sprinkle with salt and pepper and serve immediately.

cowboy caviar couscous salad

Israeli couscous is awesome. It's basically little balls of pasta (bigger than the regular couscous) that you cook by boiling and then serve with any number of mix-ins. I'm partial to using it in my go-to summer side dish of "cowboy caviar." You can serve this salad at room temperature, or chilled, or even warm.

Prep Time: 15 minutes
Total Time: 15 minutes
Serves: 6

½ cup Israeli couscous (also known as pearl couscous)
1 cup chicken stock
2 Hass avocados
1 red bell pepper
1 cup cooked and rinsed black-eyed peas
1 cup fresh corn kernels
½ cup finely diced red onion
½ cup halved cherry tomatoes
½ cup of your favorite store-bought salsa
¼ cup thinly sliced scallions
3 tablespoons chopped fresh cilantro
1 lime
1 teaspoon red pepper flakes
Coarse salt and freshly ground black pepper to taste

Put the couscous in a small saucepan with the chicken stock. Bring to a boil and then reduce the heat to medium-low and continue to cook until all the liquid has evaporated, about 10 to 12 minutes. Transfer the cooked couscous to a large bowl and let cool.

Cut each avocado in half lengthwise. Remove the pit from the avocado and discard. Remove the avocado from the skin, and dice the avocado into ½-inch pieces. Transfer to the bowl of Israeli couscous.

Dice the red bell pepper into ½-inch pieces, similar to that of the avocado. Add the red pepper to the couscous, along with the black-eyed peas, corn, red onion, cherry tomatoes, salsa, scallions, and cilantro. Toss everything together to combine. Zest and juice the lime into the salad and add the red pepper flakes. Sprinkle with salt and pepper, taste and adjust seasoning as needed, and serve immediately.

meats

It's pretty much common knowledge among my friends and family that if you're coming over to my house for dinner, you're without a doubt going to get some kind of protein and some form of avocado. It's what I do. I can't help myself. I just have no self-control when it comes to avocado. And the possibilities are endless. But let me let you in on a little secret . . . people love it! So it's safe to say that this is going to be a theme in my life for quite some time.

carnitas with chipotle guacamole

Carnitas are my signature dish. If I'm hosting a party, or trying to impress my husband's coworkers, or cooking for new friends, I almost always make carnitas. These succulent pieces of pork basically melt in your mouth and just beg to be served with a big bowl of chipotle guacamole and warm tortillas. Just add a dollop or two of guacamole to the tortilla and pile in some carnitas, then fold it up and enjoy.

Prep Time: 10 minutes
Cook Time: 2 hours 50 minutes
Total Time: 3 hours
Serves: 6 to 8

3 to 4 pounds pork shoulder, excess fat trimmed
1 medium yellow onion
1 cup fresh orange juice
¼ cup fresh lime juice
¼ cup store-bought salsa
3 garlic cloves, peeled
2 teaspoons ground cumin
2 teaspoons coarse salt
1 batch Chipotle Guacamole (page 52)
Twelve to sixteen 4-inch corn or flour tortillas

Cut the pork into 2-inch pieces and transfer to a large heavy ovenproof skillet. Cut the onion into 8 large chunks and transfer to the skillet. Add the orange juice, lime juice, salsa, garlic, cumin, and salt to the skillet and carefully stir the ingredients around to evenly distribute the liquid. Add enough water to just cover the pork and set the skillet over medium-high heat. Bring the mixture to a boil, cover, and reduce the heat to a simmer. Let it cook for 2 hours.

Remove the lid and bring the mixture back to a boil. Cook until almost all of the liquid has evaporated, about 45 minutes longer. By now the pork should be extremely tender and fall apart easily when touched with a fork.

Remove the skillet from the stove and preheat the oven to broil. Place the skillet under the broiler for 3 to 5 minutes, until the top of the pork just begins to caramelize and turn golden brown.

Using a fork, break the larger pieces up into bite-size pieces and serve the carnitas with the guacamole and tortillas.

tlayuda: mexican pizza

Exploring food cultures in new cities is one of my favorite pastimes. You can always find me searching for a city's signature dish, and that's exactly what I did last year on a food road trip through Texas. In San Antonio, we discovered the tlayuda. It's similar to a Mexican pizza and you're going to love it.

Prep Time: 10 minutes
Cook Time: 25 minutes
Total Time: 4 hours 20 minutes
Serves: 6

6   boneless, skinless chicken thighs
¾   cup chipotle salsa
1   tablespoon sweet paprika
1   tablespoon chili powder
2   teaspoons ground cumin
1   teaspoon coarse salt
½   teaspoon red pepper flakes
6   small corn tortillas
2   teaspoons extra-virgin olive oil
1   cup canned refried black beans
½   cup crumbled queso fresco
½   cup shredded Oaxaca cheese (Monterey Jack may be substituted)
1   cup shredded lettuce
1   batch Charred Corn Guacamole (page 50)

Combine the chicken thighs, salsa, paprika, chili powder, cumin, salt, and red pepper flakes in a 6½-quart slow cooker. Set the slow cooker to the high heat setting and cook the chicken for 3 to 4 hours, until the chicken is easy to shred. Remove the chicken from the slower cooker and shred using two forks. Put the chicken in a bowl and set aside.

Preheat the oven to 450°F.

Lay the corn tortillas on a baking sheet and brush both sides of the tortillas with the olive oil. Transfer the baking sheet to the oven for 5 minutes to lightly toast. Remove the baking sheet from the oven and spread 2 tablespoons of the refried beans on top of each tortilla in a thin layer. Top the tortillas with even amounts of the shredded chicken, queso fresco, and Oaxaca cheese. Transfer the baking sheet back into the oven and bake for another 5 to 7 minutes, until the cheese has melted and the tortillas are golden brown and crisp. Top with the shredded lettuce and guacamole and serve immediately.

margarita marinated pork kebabs with tomatillo-avocado salsa

I am a margarita kinda gal. They are my drink of choice no matter what the season. I think this is largely due to the fact that I grew up in Arizona, and margaritas are basically a way of life there. I'm also a huge pork fan, so the marriage of margaritas and pork seemed like a no-brainer. You simply marinate cubes of pork in my favorite homemade margarita mix and then grill! This should absolutely be enjoyed with a fresh margarita or two.

Prep Time: 15 minutes
Cook Time: 12 minutes
Total Time: 27 minutes
Serves: 2 (makes 6 skewers)

1 pound pork shoulder, excess fat trimmed and cut into 1-inch cubes (about 30 cubes)

½ cup fresh lime juice

½ cup fresh orange juice

⅓ cup extra-virgin olive oil

¼ cup chopped fresh cilantro

¼ cup tequila (any kind of tequila will work)

2 teaspoons ground cumin

1 teaspoon dried oregano

1½ teaspoons coarse salt

1 teaspoon freshly ground black pepper

1 batch Tomatillo-Avocado Salsa (page 66)

In a large bowl, combine the cubed pork, lime juice, orange juice, olive oil, cilantro, tequila, cumin, oregano, salt, and pepper. Cover the bowl tightly with plastic wrap and refrigerate for 2 to 3 hours.

Prepare a gas, charcoal, or indoor grill.

Remove the pork from the marinade and skewer the pork onto metal skewers, about 5 cubes per skewer. Grill the pork over high heat on all 4 sides for 3 minutes per side (about 12 minutes total), until the pork is cooked through. Serve immediately with the salsa.

grilled flank steak with avocado chimichurri

Each summer there comes a point when I refuse to stay inside and instead find myself poolside and by the grill during all free daylight hours. I love a good flank steak that's been marinated and is packed with flavor. Serve it with an avocado chimichurri and the creaminess from the avocado and kick from the vinegar will perfectly complement the steak!

Prep Time: 30 minutes to 2 hours (includes time to marinate the steak)
Cook Time: 8 to 10 minutes
Total Time: about 40 minutes to 2 hours 10 minutes (includes time to marinate the steak)
Serves: 2

½ cup plus 3 tablespoons extra-virgin olive oil
1 tablespoon ground cumin
2 teaspoons dried oregano
1½ teaspoons coarse salt
1 teaspoon red pepper flakes
1 pound flank steak
½ Hass avocado
1 cup firmly packed fresh parsley
2 tablespoons firmly packed fresh oregano
2 garlic cloves, peeled
1 teaspoon red wine vinegar

Mix 3 tablespoons of the olive oil, the cumin, dried oregano, 1 teaspoon of the salt, and ½ teaspoon of the red pepper flakes in a small bowl. Rub this on the flank steak and set aside in the refrigerator to marinate for at least 30 minutes and up to 2 hours.

Prepare a gas or charcoal grill.

Remove the pit from the avocado half and discard. Remove the avocado from the skin, and place the avocado flesh in the bowl of a food processor. Add the parsley, fresh oregano, garlic cloves, vinegar, the remaining ½ teaspoon salt, and remaining ½ teaspoon red pepper flakes. Pulse for 1 to 2 minutes, until the parsley is finely chopped. With the food processor whirling, drizzle in the remaining ½ cup olive oil. Taste and season with salt and pepper as needed. Set the chimichurri aside.

Grill the flank steak over medium-high heat for 2 minutes, and then rotate 90 degrees in order to achieve crossed grill marks; grill for 2 minutes more. Repeat this process on the other side of the steak and remove from the grill. About 8 minutes of grilling will result in a flank steak on the medium-rare side. Increase the grilling time if you want a more well-done steak.

Transfer the flank steak to a cutting board, tent with a piece of aluminum foil, and let rest for 10 minutes. When you are ready to serve, thinly slice the steak against the grain and serve with the chimichurri.

cheese-bellied guacamole turkey burger

Cheese-Bellied Guacamole Turkey Burgers will always be near and dear to my heart. This was the first meal I ever cooked for my husband in our first apartment together. And then I pretty much made them three times a week for the next couple of months. Each time I'd adjust a little something, and now we finally have a masterpiece! This one's so easy that even my husband will make it for us. And he doesn't usually cook!

Prep Time: 5 minutes
Cook Time: 8 to 10 minutes
Total Time: 15 minutes
Serves: 4

1¼ pounds ground turkey
1 tablespoon sweet paprika
1 tablespoon chili powder
1 teaspoon red pepper flakes
1 teaspoon garlic salt
4 ounces pepper Jack cheese, shredded
4 hamburger buns, sliced
2 teaspoons extra-virgin olive oil, plus more for brushing
1 batch Bacon-Cotija Guacamole (page 55)

Prepare a gas or charcoal grill.

In a large bowl, combine the ground turkey, paprika, chili powder, red pepper flakes, and garlic salt. Mix together with your hands until the spices are evenly incorporated. Divide the mixture into 4 equal portions.

Take 1 portion of the ground turkey and form it into a large disk. Add 1 ounce of the shredded cheese in the center of the turkey disk. Form the patty into a ball to enclose the cheese and then form the turkey into a patty that is roughly 4 inches wide and 1 inch thick. Repeat this process for the remaining turkey and transfer the 4 turkey patties to a plate.

Brush the hot grill with olive oil.

Transfer each turkey burger to the grill and cook for 4 to 5 minutes. Flip the burgers and grill for another 4 to 5 minutes, until fully cooked. Remove the patties from the grill and transfer to a clean plate.

Brush the hamburger buns with the olive oil and transfer to the grill for 1 minute, until they are just toasted.

Put 1 burger patty on the bottom layer of each bun. Top with ¼ cup or more of the guacamole and top with the remaining bun. Serve immediately.

irish nachos

It wasn't until my last two years in college that I really got into cooking. Don't get me wrong; I always liked eating. (Hello, freshman 15!) But it wasn't until my later college years when I really started to experiment in the kitchen. Irish Nachos were a creation one random Saturday night and have been around ever since. Also—single ladies beware—these have been to known to elicit proposals from whatever men you feed them to.

Prep Time: 10 minutes
Cook Time: 1 hour
Total Time: 1 hour 10 minutes
Serves: 6 to 8

4 large red-skinned potatoes
3 tablespoons extra-virgin olive oil
2 teaspoons garlic powder
2 teaspoons sweet paprika
½ red bell pepper
½ yellow bell pepper
1 medium yellow onion
Coarse salt and freshly ground black pepper to taste
5 strips bacon
2 cups shredded cheddar cheese
2 Hass avocados
½ cup thinly sliced scallions
Sour cream, for serving
Salsa, for serving

Preheat the oven to 400°F.

Using a mandoline or a very sharp knife, carefully cut the potatoes into ¼-inch-thick slices. Rinse the potatoes in cold water and drain. Arrange the potatoes on a clean kitchen towel and dry both sides.

Add the potato slices to a large bowl and drizzle with 2 tablespoons of the olive oil and the garlic powder and paprika. Toss to combine. Arrange the slices of potatoes, slightly overlapping one another, in a 12-inch cast-iron skillet. Transfer the skillet to the oven and bake the potatoes for 40 minutes, until golden brown and cooked through.

While the potatoes are baking, thinly slice the red bell pepper, yellow bell pepper, and yellow onion into ¼-inch-thick slices. Add the remaining 1 tablespoon olive oil to a large skillet over medium-high heat. Add the peppers and onions and cook, stirring occasionally, until the onions are translucent, about 5 minutes. Remove the mixture from the skillet, season with salt and pepper, and set aside.

Add the bacon to the skillet and reduce the heat to medium. Cook the bacon until golden brown and slightly crisp, turning halfway through. Transfer the bacon to a paper towel–lined plate and let cool. Break the cooked bacon into 1-inch pieces and set aside.

Once the potatoes are cooked, remove the skillet from the oven and add the pepper and onion mixture on top of the potatoes, followed by the cheese. Transfer the skillet back to the oven for 5 minutes to melt the cheese.

Once the cheese has melted, remove the skillet from the oven and sprinkle the bacon on top.

Cut each avocado in half lengthwise. Remove the pit from the avocado and discard. Remove the avocado from the skin, and place the avocado flesh in a medium bowl. Mash the avocado together with the scallions and season with salt and pepper. Add the mashed avocado on top of the nachos and serve immediately with sour cream and salsa, if desired.

Note: In order to serve this, cut it into wedges, similar to how you would cut a pie.

did you know?

On average, 53.5 million pounds of guacamole are eaten every Super Bowl Sunday, enough to cover a football field more than 20 feet thick.

carne asada fries

I'm fairly certain these fries are one of the reasons I'm married. They are the epitome of man food. First, they are loaded with meat. Second, they are messy. Third, they are most definitely meant to be eaten as finger food, in front of the TV, on game day. I'll whip these up for my hubby anytime there's a big game and he is all smiles.

Prep Time: 4 to 6 hours
Cook Time: 50 to 60 minutes
Total Time: 5 to 7 hours
Serves: 4 to 6

1   orange
1   lime
½   cup chopped fresh cilantro
¼   cup plus 1 tablespoon extra-virgin olive oil
2   tablespoons chopped jalapeño chile pepper
2   garlic cloves, smashed
1   teaspoon coarse salt
1   pound flank steak
3   russet potatoes (about 3 pounds)
1   teaspoon garlic salt
1   teaspoon onion flakes
½   teaspoon ground cumin
½   teaspoon freshly ground black pepper
2   cups shredded Colby-Jack cheese
1   cup pico de gallo
1   batch Tomatillo-Avocado Salsa (page 66)

Zest and juice the orange into a large bowl. Zest and juice the lime into the same bowl. Add the cilantro, ¼ cup of the olive oil, the jalapeño, garlic, and salt to the bowl and stir to combine.

Put the flank steak in a zip-top plastic bag and add the marinade mixture on top. Remove any excess air from the plastic bag and zip the top closed. Transfer the steak to the fridge for 4 to 6 hours to marinate.

About 45 minutes before your steak is done marinating, start to prepare the potatoes.

Preheat the oven to 425°F.

Peel the potatoes and slice into thick, long wedges. Each potato should yield about 8 wedges. Put the wedges into a zip-top plastic bag and add the garlic salt, onion flakes, cumin, black pepper, and remaining 1 tablespoon olive oil. Zip the top of the bag closed and give the bag a gentle shake to coat the potatoes with the seasoning.

Spread the potatoes on a parchment-lined baking sheet and bake for 20 minutes. Flip the potatoes over and bake for another 20 to 25 minutes, until they are golden brown. Let cool slightly.

Prepare a gas or charcoal grill.

Remove the steak from the marinade and grill over medium-high heat for 2 minutes, then rotate 90 degrees in order to achieve crossed grill marks and cook for 2 minutes more. Repeat this process on the other side of the steak and remove from the grill. About 8 minutes of grilling will result in a flank steak on the medium-rare side. Increase the grilling time if you want a more well-done steak.

Transfer the flank steak to a cutting board, tent it with a piece of aluminum foil, and let rest for 10 minutes. Cut the carne asada into thin slices against the grain and then chop into 1-inch pieces.

Arrange the potato wedges on a large ovenproof serving platter. Top with the shredded cheese and melt the cheese in the oven for 3 to 5 minutes. Top the cheesy fries with the chopped carne asada. Drizzle the pico de gallo on top and then dollop with the salsa. Serve immediately.

fish

Avocado and fish is a match made in heaven—you can't go wrong with this pairing. Whether you are using a flaky and buttery mahi mahi or a dense and meatier swordfish, avocado makes the perfect companion for these dishes. I love serving fish with a big dollop of guacamole or avocado relish on top, or subbing in some mashed-up avocado in place of mayonnaise in a classic lobster roll. Whichever way you spin it, avocado and fish are perfect for each other.

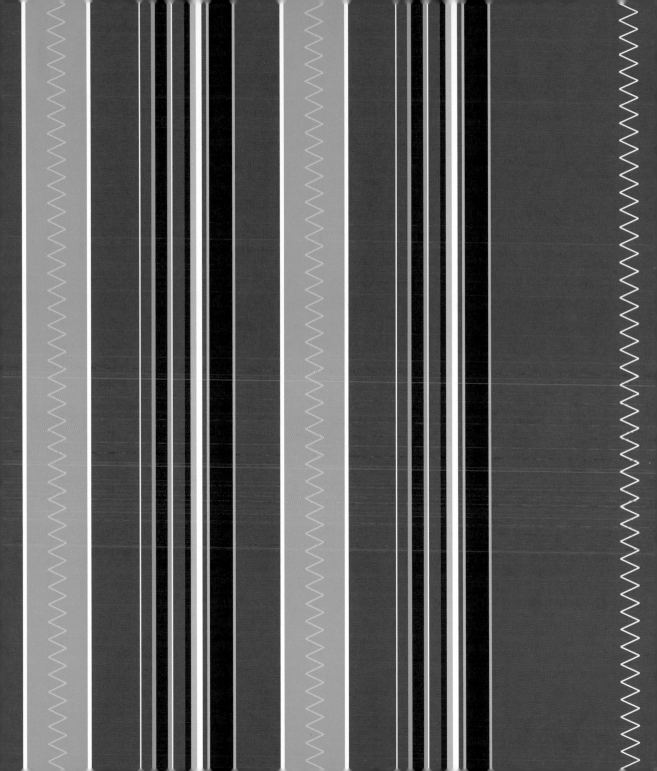

pan-seared salmon with avocado-pepper relish

Growing up as a picky eater, I was skeptical when it came time to finally try salmon when I got in culinary school. But I have no idea what the heck I was thinking, because now I can't get enough of this gorgeous pink fish. It's by far one of my favorite dishes, and I love a good crispy crust with plenty of citrus to squeeze on top. The avocado-pepper relish is both crunchy and packed with citrus, and it's the perfect addition to this meal.

Prep Time: 10 minutes
Cook Time: 15 minutes
Total Time: 25 minutes
Serves: 4

2 Hass avocados
½ cup chopped red bell pepper, ¼-inch dice
½ cup chopped yellow bell pepper, ¼-inch dice
3 tablespoons extra-virgin olive oil
2 tablespoons finely chopped fresh chives
2 tablespoons finely chopped jalapeño chile pepper
1½ tablespoons fresh lime juice
Coarse salt and freshly ground black pepper to taste
4 8-ounce skin-on salmon filets
Lemon wedges, for serving

Cut each avocado in half lengthwise. Remove the pit from the avocado and discard. Remove the avocado from the skin, and carefully dice the avocado into ½-inch cubes. Transfer to a medium bowl. Add the chopped red and yellow bell peppers, 1 tablespoon of the olive oil, the chives, jalapeño, and lime juice. Carefully mix together and taste and season with the salt and pepper as needed.

Heat a large skillet over medium-high heat until almost smoking. Season the salmon filets with salt and pepper on both sides and the remaining 2 tablespoons olive oil. Transfer to the hot skillet, skin side down. Cook the filets for 4 to 5 minutes on each side, until just lightly pink in the center.

Serve immediately with equal portions of the avocado-pepper relish and a wedge of lemon.

crab cakes with basil-avocado aioli

Is there anything better than a light, fluffy, golden crab cake dipped in a spiced avocado-based aioli sauce? I don't think so. These crab cakes are going to make you wish you lived on the coast, where you could catch fresh crab on a daily basis. And this basil-avocado aioli is going to have you begging for more! Don't be surprised if you start whipping it up for other things too, like a big pile of freshly made french fries!

Prep Time: 15 minutes
Cook Time: 15 minutes
Total Time: 30 minutes
Serves: 4
(makes 8 crab cakes)

2 Hass avocados
¼ cup sour cream
1 jalapeño chile pepper, seeds removed
¼ cup packed chopped basil
¼ cup fresh lemon juice
1 garlic clove
  Coarse salt and freshly ground black pepper to taste
⅓ cup minced scallions
¼ cup light mayonnaise
2 large eggs, lightly beaten
2 tablespoons finely chopped fresh chives
1 tablespoon grated lemon zest
1 pound lump crabmeat, drained
1 cup panko bread crumbs
¼ cup extra-virgin olive oil

Preheat the oven to 350°F.

Cut each avocado in half lengthwise. Remove the pit from the avocado and discard. Remove the avocado from the skin, and place the avocado flesh in the bowl of a food processor. Add the sour cream, jalapeño, basil, 2 tablespoons of the lemon juice, and the garlic to the bowl. Pulse for 1 to 2 minutes, until smooth and creamy. Taste and season with salt and pepper as needed and set the aioli aside.

In a large bowl, combine the scallions, mayonnaise, eggs, chives, remaining 2 tablespoons lemon juice, the lemon zest, ½ teaspoon salt, and ½ teaspoon pepper with a fork. Add the crabmeat and panko bread crumbs and toss together gently with your hands.

Form the crab cakes by shaping a heaping ¼ cup of the crab mixture into a 3½-inch disk, about 1½ inches thick, making 8 cakes. Set the shaped crab cakes on a plate.

Heat the olive oil in a large skillet over medium-high heat. Add 4 crab cakes at a time and cook for 2 to 3 minutes on each side, until golden brown. Repeat this process for the remaining crab cakes.

Serve immediately with the basil-avocado aioli for dipping.

grilled swordfish with spicy avocado sauce

Swordfish is most definitely a meatier type of fish. It's not light like halibut or sea bass, so it definitely needs something that can stand up to its texture. This spicy avocado sauce is the perfect accessory for this meal. The creaminess from the avocado and the spiciness from the red jalapeño pepper create the perfect balance with the swordfish.

Prep Time: 10 minutes
Cook Time: 8 minutes
Total Time: 18 minutes
Serves: 4
(makes 1 cup sauce)

1 Hass avocado
2 tablespoons fresh lime juice
2 teaspoons honey
½ red jalapeño chile pepper, seeded
Coarse salt and freshly ground black pepper to taste
2 tablespoons extra-virgin olive oil
1 tablespoon fresh lemon juice
4 8-ounce swordfish steaks, cut 1 inch thick
2 large handfuls arugula

Prepare a gas or charcoal grill.

Cut the avocado in half lengthwise. Remove the pit from the avocado and discard. Remove the avocado from the skin, and place the avocado flesh in the bowl of a food processor. Add the lime juice, honey, and red jalapeño to the food processor. Pulse for 1 to 2 minutes, until smooth and creamy. Taste and season with the salt and pepper as needed. Set the sauce aside.

Combine the olive oil and lemon juice in a small bowl. Dip each piece of swordfish into the lemon–olive oil mixture. Season both sides of the swordfish with salt and pepper. Transfer to the grill over high heat and cook for 3 to 4 minutes per side, until opaque and fully cooked.

Arrange the arugula on a serving platter and place the grilled swordfish on top. Drizzle the spicy avocado sauce over the swordfish steaks and serve immediately.

cumin-dusted mahi mahi tacos

I feel like mahi mahi gets the short end of the stick. Unless I'm in Hawaii or a taco shop in Los Angeles, I rarely see this light and flavorful fish on a menu. I like to make a cumin-scented marinade that the fish can soak in for a few minutes before getting cooked. Then I pile the flaky fish into a taco and smother it with the best tomatillo-avocado salsa in the entire world. Done and done.

Prep Time: 25 minutes
(includes time to marinate the fish)
Cook Time: 10 minutes
Total Time: 35 minutes
(includes time to marinate the fish)
Serves: 4 (makes 8 tacos)

4   4-ounce skinless mahi mahi filets
1   lime
4   teaspoons extra-virgin olive oil
½   teaspoon sweet paprika
½   teaspoon ground cumin
    Coarse salt and freshly ground black pepper to taste
8   4-inch flour or corn tortillas
1   cup shredded lettuce
½   cup pico de gallo
1   batch Tomatillo-Avocado Salsa (page 66)

Arrange the mahi mahi in a small baking dish.

Zest and juice the lime into a small bowl. Add 2 teaspoons of the olive oil, the paprika, and cumin to the bowl and stir together. Pour the spice marinade over the fish and let sit for 20 minutes.

Heat a large skillet over medium-high heat with the remaining 2 teaspoons of olive oil. Sprinkle the mahi mahi with salt and pepper, put the fish in the skillet, and cook until the outside is golden brown and the fish is flaky and cooked through, 3 to 5 minutes per side. Transfer the mahi mahi to a cutting board. Using a fork, gently flake the fish into bite size pieces.

Wrap the tortillas in a damp paper towel and microwave for 45 seconds, until warm.

To assemble, add about ¼ cup of the mahi mahi to the center of each tortilla, along with some shredded lettuce. Add 1 tablespoon pico de gallo, drizzle with 1 to 2 tablespoons of the salsa, and serve.

grilled shrimp & avocado pasta

Back when I lived in Tucson, we would go up to our country club every Wednesday night for Italian night. Being the predictable eater I was as a child, I would order the same things every time. Linguine with a light olive oil and garlic sauce and extra Parmesan cheese, please. This pasta dish is a sassy version of my childhood favorite. The avocado-Parmesan sauce gives the pasta a light coating of flavor and the garlicky shrimp are just downright addictive.

Prep Time: 10 minutes
Cook Time: 15 minutes
Total Time: 25 minutes
Serves: 6

1 ripe Hass avocado
2 tablespoons grated Parmesan cheese, plus more for serving (optional)
1 tablespoon fresh lemon juice
¼ cup extra-virgin olive oil
Coarse salt and freshly ground black pepper to taste
1 pound linguine
2 tablespoons butter
2 tablespoons minced garlic
1 pound medium shrimp, peeled and deveined
¼ cup chopped scallions
1 teaspoon red pepper flakes

Cut the avocado in half lengthwise. Remove the pit from the avocado and discard. Remove the avocado from the skin, and place the avocado in the bowl of a food processor. Add the Parmesan and lemon juice to the food processor bowl. Pulse the mixture for 1 to 2 minutes while streaming in 2 tablespoons of the olive oil until smooth and creamy. Scrape down the sides of the food processor bowl with a spatula as needed. Season the sauce with salt and pepper. Set the avocado mixture aside.

Bring a large pot of water to a boil. Add the linguine and cook according to the package directions. Once the pasta is al dente, drain the pasta.

Add the butter and remaining 2 tablespoons olive oil to a large skillet over medium heat. Add the garlic and cook for 30 seconds. Add the shrimp and cook until they are pink and cooked through, about 2 minutes per side. Add the scallions and red pepper flakes and stir to combine. Add the cooked pasta and the avocado-Parmesan sauce to the shrimp mixture and toss to combine using a pair of kitchen tongs. The pasta should be evenly coated with the avocado-Parmesan mixture. Taste and adjust seasoning as needed.

Serve immediately, with more Parmesan if desired.

did you know?

Avocados have one of the highest protein content of any fruit.

avocado tuna ceviche

Remember those sesame crackers I told you about a few chapters back? Well, they are just the perfect vehicles for this ceviche made with tuna and avocado. We've got an amazing fish market here in Santa Monica, and my fishmongers always advise me on what's fresh and delicious. So when they told me I had to try the sashimi-grade tuna they had just gotten in, I said why not! A few minutes later it was marinating in soy sauce, sesame oil, rice vinegar, and a bit of serrano pepper. Voilà . . . ceviche.

Prep Time: 10 minutes
Total Time: 20 minutes
Serves: 6

1   Hass avocado
8   ounces sushi-grade ahi tuna
2   tablespoons soy sauce
1   tablespoon toasted sesame oil
½   tablespoon rice vinegar
1   teaspoon finely chopped
    serrano chile pepper
    Juice of 1 lime
    Sesame crackers, for serving
1   teaspoon black sesame seeds

Cut the avocado in half lengthwise. Remove the pit from the avocado and discard. Remove the avocado from the skin, and cut the avocado into ½-inch pieces. Set aside.

Using a sharp knife, cut the tuna into ½-inch pieces.

In a large bowl, whisk together the soy sauce, sesame oil, rice vinegar, serrano pepper, and lime juice. Add the avocado and tuna to the mixture and let it sit for 10 minutes.

Top the sesame crackers with about a tablespoon of the tuna ceviche and a sprinkling of the sesame seeds. Serve immediately.

healthier avocado lobster roll

One of my favorite things about heading back East in the summer months is the obscene amount of lobster rolls that I'll consume in just a few short days. I never cease to feel guilty about the amount of calories I'm eating, but these Healthier Avocado Lobster Rolls have way less guilt, so I can make them at home and still feel good! By replacing the mayo in the lobster mixture with smashed avocado, you not only cut the calories, but you also get avocado in a lobster roll! Ummmm, yes please.

Prep Time: 10 minutes
Cook Time: 5 minutes
Total Time: 15 minutes
Serves: 4

4   hot dog rolls
4   teaspoons butter, at room
     temperature
1   Hass avocado
3   teaspoons fresh lemon juice
1   pound cooked lobster meat
1   stalk celery
     Coarse salt and freshly
       ground black pepper to taste
     Pinch of sweet paprika

Preheat the oven to broil.

Spread the hot dog rolls with the butter and lay them on a baking sheet. Transfer the baking sheet to the broiler for 3 to 4 minutes, until the hot dog buns are nicely toasted. Set the buns aside.

Cut the avocado in half lengthwise. Remove the pit from the avocado and discard. Remove the avocado from the skin, and place the flesh in the bowl of a food processor. Add the lemon juice and pulse for 2 minutes, until smooth. Transfer the avocado mixture to a large bowl.

Chop the lobster meat into bite-size pieces, about ¾ inch each, and add to the bowl with the avocado.

Trim the ends of the celery and finely mince the celery. Add the celery to the bowl with the avocado and lobster mixture. Toss everything together to combine. Taste the mixture and season with salt and pepper as needed.

Put one-quarter of the mixture into each toasted hot dog bun. Sprinkle a pinch of paprika over the top of each avocado lobster roll and serve immediately.

vegetarian

Growing up in a mostly vegetarian house meant one amazing thing . . . lots and lots of pasta. I was a pasta freak. My grandparents used to tell me that I would turn into one big carb if I didn't expand my horizons and start trying other things. Well, look at me now! We are by no means vegetarian, but I'll cook veggie-based meals a few times a week, and we love it. Quinoa, farro, pasta of course, mushrooms, and sweet potatoes are big winners in my house, and I love dressing up these simple foods with avocado to make an extraordinary meal.

balsamic portobello topped with herbed avocado salad

In one of our early culinary school classes, we were tasked with preparing a dish with an ingredient we had never used before. So I, being the picky eater I used to be, grabbed a bag of wild mushrooms and headed off to make a mushroom risotto. My awesome culinary school instructor and chef looked at me like I was a lunatic for not having had mushrooms before. Since that day, though, I have been a mushroom fanatic. These balsamic baked portobellos have just the right amount of tang from the balsamic vinegar to pair with a creamy herbed avocado salad.

Prep Time: 5 minutes
Cook Time: 35 minutes
Total Time: 40 minutes
Serves: 4

¼ cup balsamic vinegar
4 portobello mushroom caps
1 tablespoon extra-virgin olive oil
Coarse salt and freshly ground black pepper to taste
2 Hass avocados
¾ cup thinly sliced scallions
⅓ cup crumbled feta cheese
¼ cup finely chopped fresh chives
2 tablespoons finely chopped fresh dill
Juice of ½ lemon (about 1 tablespoon)

Preheat the oven to 400°F.

Bring the vinegar to a boil in a small saucepan. Cook until the vinegar has reduced by half, 3 to 5 minutes.

Arrange the portobello mushrooms on a parchment-lined baking sheet, gill side up. Drizzle the mushrooms with the olive oil and sprinkle with salt and pepper. Transfer the baking sheet to the oven and bake for 20 minutes, until the mushrooms are tender. Drizzle the mushrooms with the reduced vinegar and bake for another 10 minutes.

While the mushrooms are baking, cut each avocado in half lengthwise. Remove the pit from the avocado and discard. Remove the avocado from the skin, and cut each half into large dice. Transfer the avocado to a medium bowl. Mix in the scallions, feta, chives, dill, and lemon juice. Carefully toss to combine. Season with salt and pepper as needed.

Top the mushrooms with equal amounts of the herbed avocado salad. Serve immediately.

fried avocado tacos

For my twenty-fifth birthday, my food blogging friends took me on a taco-and-tequila bike crawl through Austin, Texas. We must have had about 10 tacos throughout the day, but nothing even came close to the first taco we tried: a fried avocado taco. I basically melted when I read those words on the menu. Say whaaaat?! Fried avocado? I think I just died and went to heaven. These are basically the best tacos ever served in Austin, but since I can't up and move there, I've moved the tacos to Los Angeles so that I get the best of both worlds!

Prep Time: 10 minutes
Cook Time: 10 minutes
Total Time: 2 hours 20 minutes
Serves: 4

½ cup pale ale
½ cup all-purpose flour
1 teaspoon sweet paprika
½ teaspoon ground cumin
¼ teaspoon cayenne pepper
½ teaspoon coarse salt
2 cups grapeseed oil (or other
    neutral oil), for frying
2 Hass avocados
8 small corn tortillas
1 cup refried beans, warmed
1 cup store-bought salsa verde
½ cup shredded Mexican cheese
½ cup sour cream mixed with
    1 teaspoon sauce from can of
    chipotle chile peppers, for
    garnish

Whisk together the pale ale, flour, paprika, cumin, cayenne pepper, and salt. Cover the mixture with plastic wrap and let sit for 2 hours.

Heat the grapeseed oil in a tall pot over medium high heat until about 375°F.

Cut each avocado in half lengthwise. Remove the pit from the avocado and discard. Remove the avocado from the skin and cut each half into 4 pieces. Dredge each avocado piece in the beer batter, gently transfer it to the hot oil, and fry until golden brown, 1 to 2 minutes. You can fry a few pieces at a time; just be careful not to overcrowd the oil. Remove the avocado with a slotted spoon and set on a paper towel–lined plate to drain. Repeat this process with the remaining avocado pieces.

Wrap the corn tortillas in a damp paper towel and heat for 1 minute in the microwave or by quickly holding them with tongs over a stovetop flame for about 15 seconds on each side, until they are just fragrant.

Arrange the corn tortillas on a platter. Evenly divide the refried beans among the tortillas, followed by the salsa verde, a few slices of the fried avocado, and the cheese. Serve immediately with the chipotle-infused sour cream.

mozzarella & farro salad

My mom's a vegetarian, so I'm always on the hunt for fun new vegetarian dishes that I can wow her with when she is in town to visit. This salad is one of her favorites. The herby dressing that coats the cooked farro and fresh mozzarella makes this dish completely unforgettable, even for a meat lover!

Prep Time: 10 minutes
Cook Time: 25 minutes
Total Time: 35 minutes
Serves: 6

1½ cups semi-pearled farro
4 cups water
1 Hass avocado
1 cup halved cherry tomatoes
1 cup small halved mozzarella balls
½ cup extra-virgin olive oil
2 tablespoons red wine vinegar
1 tablespoon grainy Dijon mustard
1 tablespoon grated Parmesan cheese
1 teaspoon dried oregano
1 teaspoon dried parsley
1 teaspoon minced garlic
½ teaspoon minced shallots
¼ teaspoon coarse salt
¼ teaspoon freshly ground black pepper
2 cups arugula

Combine the farro and the water in a medium stockpot. Bring the water to a boil and then reduce to a simmer and cook until all the liquid has evaporated, about 25 minutes. Transfer the cooked farro to a colander and rinse with cold water. Transfer the drained farro to a bowl and stir to prevent the farro from sticking.

Cut the avocado in half lengthwise. Remove the pit from the avocado and discard. Remove the avocado from the skin, and cut the avocado into ½-inch pieces. Transfer to the bowl with the farro, and add the cherry tomatoes and mozzarella.

In a large bowl, combine the olive oil, vinegar, mustard, Parmesan, oregano, parsley, garlic, shallots, salt, and pepper. Whisk everything to combine. Drizzle the vinaigrette over the farro and stir to combine. Taste and adjust salt and pepper as needed.

Arrange the arugula on a large platter. Top with the farro mixture and serve immediately.

did you know?

Avocados contain more potassium than bananas.

mediterranean avocado pizza

I've been having homemade pizza night every week since college. It's usually on Tuesday, and I just throw together a fun and new pizza creation with whatever we have on hand from the market that week. This Mediterranean-inspired pizza is light but totally filling and packed with flavor. The red onion, sun-dried tomatoes, and avocado are perfect along with the pesto and goat cheese. It's a savory dish you'll want to keep on hand for vegetarians when you're doing pizza night.

Prep Time: 10 minutes
Cook Time: 12 minutes
Total Time: 22 minutes
Serves: 8

1 pound store-bought pizza dough, whole wheat preferred
⅓ cup store-bought pesto
3 ounces goat cheese
3 tablespoons chopped sun-dried tomatoes in oil
¼ cup thinly sliced red onion
1 Hass avocado
Coarse salt and freshly ground black pepper to taste

Preheat the oven to 475°F.

On a lightly floured baking sheet, stretch the pizza dough out to fill the entire sheet.

Using the back of a spoon, spread the pesto on the pizza dough. Evenly distribute the goat cheese by putting small spoonfuls of the cheese on top of the pesto, followed by the chopped sun-dried tomatoes and the red onion. Transfer the baking sheet into the oven and bake for 10 to 12 minutes, until the crust is golden brown and the cheese slightly melts.

Cut the avocado in half lengthwise. Remove the pit from the avocado and discard. Remove the avocado from the skin, and cut ⅓-inch-thick slices from the avocado. Lay them evenly on top of the pizza. Sprinkle with salt and pepper and serve immediately.

sweet potato burgers

When I was growing up in a mostly vegetarian house, we had a lot of veggie burgers. Now don't get me wrong, I love my mom's lentil burger, but there's something about a veggie burger with sweet potatoes that really gets me going. These sweet potato burgers are light and fresh, and the flavors just pop because of the lemon zest.

Prep Time: 15 minutes
Cook Time: 8 to 10 minutes
Total Time: 25 minutes
Serves: 4

1   cup peeled and diced sweet potatoes
1   15-ounce can cannellini beans, rinsed and drained
1½ cups panko bread crumbs
1   large egg
2   tablespoons grated Parmesan cheese
1   tablespoon grated lemon zest
1   teaspoon coarse salt
½   teaspoon freshly ground black pepper
½   teaspoon sweet paprika
½   teaspoon dried oregano
2   tablespoons extra-virgin olive oil
4   hamburger buns, sliced and toasted
2   Hass avocados
    Assorted toppings, such as red onions, roasted red bell peppers, microgreens, Dijon mustard, lettuce, sun-dried tomatoes, and/or caramelized onions

Bring a small pot of water to a boil. Add the diced sweet potatoes and cook until fork-tender, 5 to 7 minutes. Drain the sweet potatoes and transfer to the bowl of a food processor. Add the cannellini beans, bread crumbs, egg, Parmesan, lemon zest, salt, pepper, paprika, and oregano. Pulse for 1 minute, until everything is fully incorporated and smooth.

Remove the sweet potato mixture from the food processor and divide it into four 4-ounce portions. Form each portion into a patty to fit your preferred burger bun.

Heat the olive oil in a large skillet over medium-high heat. Add the sweet potato patties to the hot oil and cook until golden brown, 4 to 5 minutes per side. Transfer each patty to a burger bun bottom.

Cut each avocado in half lengthwise. Remove the pit from the avocado and discard. Remove the avocado from the skin, and cut the avocado into thin strips. Top each sweet potato patty with one-quarter of the avocado strips. Add additional toppings as desired and top with the top half of the bun. Serve immediately.

herbed quinoa & avocado stuffed peppers

Whenever my Omi and Papa would come visit us in Arizona, they would always make stuffed peppers. I can distinctly remember coming home from school or tennis practice and knowing what we were having for dinner before I even walked in the door. Stuffed peppers just have a way of making the entire house smell like my grandparents' home in Florida. It is always such a treat to have Omi and Papa cook for us! Their stuffed pepper recipe is one of my favorites. They have made these countless times with stuffings ranging from meat to rice to vegetables. My latest rendition is stuffed with quinoa and avocado. Obviously!

Prep Time: 10 minutes
Cook Time: 70 minutes
Total Time: 80 minutes
Serves: 4

4   red or yellow bell peppers
1   cup quinoa
2½ cups vegetable stock
½   cup crumbled feta cheese
½   cup canned tomato puree
¼   cup finely chopped fresh
    parsley
2   tablespoons finely chopped
    fresh chives
2   tablespoons finely chopped
    fresh dill
1   Hass avocado
    Coarse salt and freshly
    ground black pepper to taste
1   28-ounce can crushed
    tomatoes

Cut the tops off the bell peppers and carefully remove the seeds and the white membranes from the pepper while making sure to leave the pepper intact. Reserve the tops and the hollowed-out peppers while you prepare the stuffing.

In a medium pot, combine the quinoa and vegetable stock. Bring to a boil and then reduce to a simmer and cook until the quinoa has absorbed all of the liquid, about 15 minutes. Remove the pot from the heat and let cool. Transfer the quinoa to a large bowl and toss together with the feta, tomato puree, parsley, chives, and dill.

Cut the avocado in half lengthwise. Remove the pit from the avocado and discard. Remove the avocado from the skin and cut each half of the avocado into ½-inch chunks. Add to the quinoa mixture. Toss the quinoa mixture to combine and season with salt and pepper as needed.

With a large spoon, fill each pepper to the top with the quinoa mixture. Put the top, or the "hat" of the pepper, back on top.

Add the crushed tomatoes to a 4-inch-deep skillet. Transfer the stuffed peppers to the crushed tomatoes so they are standing upright. You can snuggle them close together so they can lean on each other for support.

Bring the crushed tomatoes to a boil and then reduce to a simmer and cover. Cook until the bell peppers are fork-tender, about 45 minutes.

Remove the stuffed peppers from the crushed tomatoes and transfer to a serving platter. Spoon some of the crushed tomatoes on top and serve immediately.

vegetarian avocado sushi bowl

This is my go-to dish when I'm home alone. It's simple, clean, and filling without being too heavy. Inspired by my favorite vegetarian sushi roll in Los Angeles, this simple rice bowl is perfect for ladies' night in! And it's simple enough for even the fussiest eater.

Prep Time: 15 minutes
Cook Time: 15 to 20 minutes
Total Time: 35 minutes
Serves: 4

1 cup sushi rice
1 Hass avocado
1 cup shredded green cabbage (savoy recommended)
½ cup chopped red bell pepper
½ cup thinly sliced carrots
¼ cup finely sliced scallions
3 tablespoons chopped fresh chives
3 tablespoons soy sauce
2 tablespoons rice vinegar
1 teaspoon sesame oil
1 teaspoon honey

Cook the sushi rice according to the package directions. Transfer it to a large bowl. Cover the rice with a slightly damp kitchen towel and set aside.

Cut the avocado in half lengthwise. Remove the pit from the avocado and discard. Remove the avocado from the skin, and cut the avocado into ½-inch dice. Transfer to a large bowl. Add the cabbage, red bell pepper, carrots, scallions, and chives to the avocado and toss to combine.

In a small bowl, whisk together the soy sauce, rice vinegar, sesame oil, and honey.

Fluff the sushi rice with a fork. Add the chopped vegetable mixture and drizzle with the prepared dressing. Divide among bowls and serve immediately.

dessert

I know what you might be thinking: Avocado in desserts? Huh? I know, I know. I was once skeptical, too, but it's really quite amazing. Not only is avocado an awesome butter substitute, but it also gives a great creamy consistency to your sweets. Not to mention the fact that you will totally cut back your saturated fat intake and instead replace it with healthy fats, vitamins, and minerals. It will make your desserts a bit chewier and softer—and who doesn't love a great chewy-gooey chocolate chip cookie!

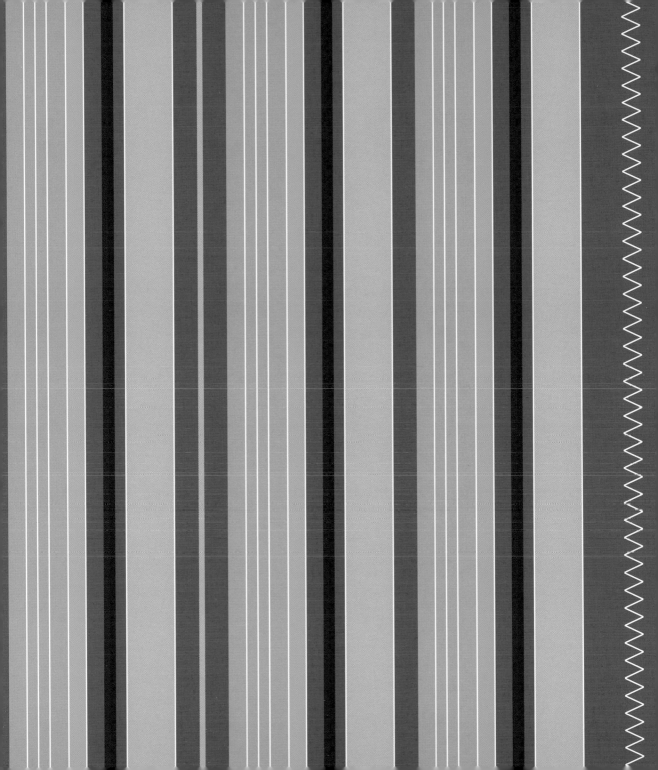

avocado chocolate chip cookies

Chocolate chip cookies are my weakness. I just can't say no, especially when they are about 10 minutes out of the oven and are still warm and gooey on the inside. Subbing the avocado for most of the butter in these cookies not only makes them healthier, but it also means that you can eat more because you won't feel quite so guilty! Cha-ching!

Prep Time: 1 hour 10 minutes (includes chilling time)
Cook Time: 18 to 20 minutes per baking sheet
Total Time: 2 hours 10 minutes
Serves: 18 (makes 3 dozen cookies)

1   Hass avocado (4½ ounces)
½   cup (1 stick) unsalted butter, at room temperature
1½ cups dark brown sugar
2   large eggs, at room temperature
2   teaspoons pure vanilla extract
2   cups all-purpose flour
1   teaspoon baking soda
1   teaspoon coarse salt
½   teaspoon baking powder
1½ cups old-fashioned rolled oats
1¾ cups semisweet chocolate chips

Cut the avocado in half lengthwise. Remove the pit from the avocado and discard. Remove the avocado from the skin and place the avocado flesh in a large bowl along with the butter and brown sugar. Cream together the avocado, butter, and sugar for 3 minutes, until fluffy.

Add the eggs one at a time, followed by the vanilla extract, scraping down the sides of the bowl as needed. Add the flour, baking soda, salt, and baking powder and slowly combine, making sure not to overmix the batter. Add the oats and chocolate chips and combine. Refrigerate the batter for 1 hour.

Preheat the oven to 325°F. Line a baking sheet with parchment paper.

Using a 2 tablespoon scoop, scoop the batter onto a clean surface and, using wet hands, roll the dough into 12 balls. Flatten the cookies with the palm of your hand to create 2½-inch disks. Arrange the 12 disks on the baking sheet. Transfer the sheet to the top rack of the oven and bake for 18 to 20 minutes, until the cookies are slightly golden brown on the edges but still soft in the middle. Remove from the oven and let rest on the baking sheet for at least 3 minutes before transferring the cookies to cooling racks. Repeat the process for remaining dough. You will bake 3 baking sheets total.

Serve the cookies immediately or store in an airtight container in the refrigerator for 5 days or in the freezer for up to 3 weeks.

avocado & chocolate chip banana bread

Growing up, my sister and I had banana bread almost every morning for breakfast. So when I figured out that I could sub the avocado for butter in my favorite cookie recipe, what was stopping me from subbing it in my favorite banana bread recipe? Don't let the slightly green batter fool you, these will bake up perfectly.

Prep Time: 10 minutes
Cook Time: 70 to 80 minutes
Total Time: About 1 hour 40 minutes
(includes cooling time)
Serves: 10

3 ounces avocado flesh
   (approximately ⅓ cup of
   mashed avocado)
¼ cup plain yogurt
½ cup granulated sugar
½ cup light brown sugar
2 large eggs
3 overripe bananas (about
   15 ounces)
2 teaspoons pure vanilla
   extract
2 cups all-purpose flour
1 teaspoon baking soda
½ teaspoon coarse salt
   Pinch of ground cinnamon
½ cup mini chocolate chips

Preheat the oven to 350°F. Spray a 9 x 4-inch loaf pan with non-stick cooking spray.

Add the avocado and yogurt to the bowl of a stand mixer and mix together until smooth. Add both sugars to the bowl with the avocado mixture and cream together for 2 to 3 minutes. Add the eggs, one at a time, scraping down the sides of the bowl between each addition. Add the bananas and vanilla extract and mix until smooth.

Add the flour, baking soda, salt, and cinnamon and mix until just combined. Stir in the chocolate chips.

Transfer the batter to the prepared loaf pan and bake for 70 to 80 minutes, or until a knife inserted in the center comes out clean. Let cool on a wire rack for 20 minutes before slicing and serving. Carefully remove the loaf from the pan before serving, once cooled.

avocado & chocolate chip pound cake

I had to do it. I just needed to create a green baked dessert. And pound cake was the answer. I've eaten a lot of pound cake in my day, and there is a lot of pound cake in my foreseeable future, so it's nice to know that I can sub out half of the butter for avocado. It cuts down on calories and saturated fat but still results in a delectable pound cake that would impress even a pastry chef!

Prep Time: 10 minutes
Cook Time: 65 minutes
Total Time: 1 hour 45 minutes
(including cooling time)
Serves: 10

1   Hass avocado (4½ ounces)
½   cup (1 stick) unsalted butter, at room temperature
1¼ cups sugar
4   large eggs
2   tablespoons buttermilk
1   tablespoon pure vanilla extract
2   cups all-purpose flour
¾   teaspoon baking soda
1   cup mini chocolate chips

Preheat the oven to 325°F. Spray a 9 x 4-inch loaf pan with nonstick cooking spray.

Cut the avocado in half lengthwise. Remove the pit from the avocado and discard. Remove the avocado from the skin and place the avocado flesh in the bowl of a stand mixer. Add the butter and sugar to the bowl with the avocado and cream together for 2 to 3 minutes. Add the eggs, one at a time, scraping down the sides of the bowl between each addition. Add the buttermilk and vanilla and mix until combined.

Add the flour and baking soda and mix until just combined. Stir in the chocolate chips with a spatula.

Transfer the batter to the prepared loaf pan and bake for 65 minutes, or until a knife inserted in the center comes out clean. Let cool for 30 minutes before slicing and serving.

avocado brownies

My grandma makes the best brownies. I've attempted to make them at home and they are, never quite the same. It's just something about grandma's baking that makes them special. The only downside is that I often eat about half the pan in one sitting. I just can't help it. But I've solved my problem. By using an avocado instead of most of the butter, I can not only sit down and eat half the pan, but I also won't feel quite as guilty about it!

Prep Time: 10 minutes
Cook Time: 35 minutes
Total Time: 1 hour 45 minutes
(including cooling time)
Serves: 10 to 15

1   Hass avocado (4½ ounces)
2   cups granulated sugar
½   cup unsweetened Dutch-
     processed cocoa powder
4   tablespoons (½ stick) unsalted
     butter
2   large eggs
1   tablespoon instant espresso
     powder
2   teaspoons pure vanilla
     extract
1   teaspoon coarse salt
1   cup all-purpose flour
⅓   cup chocolate chips
2   tablespoons confectioners'
     sugar (optional)

Preheat the oven to 350°F. Spray a 13 x 9-inch baking dish with non-stick cooking spray.

Cut the avocado in half lengthwise. Remove the pit from the avocado and discard. Remove the avocado from the skin, and place the avocado flesh in a bowl of a stand mixer. Using a paddle attachment, mix until the avocado is mashed and smooth, scraping down the sides as needed. Add the granulated sugar and beat until fully incorporated.

In a double boiler over simmering water, melt the cocoa powder and butter together until smooth. Remove the mixture from the heat and let cool.

Add the chocolate mixture to the stand mixer bowl and mix until the chocolate is fully incorporated.

Add the eggs one at a time, scraping down the sides of the bowl as needed, followed by the espresso powder, vanilla extract, and salt.

Add the flour and mix until there are no streaks of flour showing. Stir in the chocolate chips with a spatula.

Transfer the batter to the prepared baking dish and bake for 30 to 35 minutes. The brownies will be dense and moist. Let cool for at least 1 hour before slicing and serving. Dust with confectioners' sugar just before serving, if desired.

avocado-coconut ice cream

I know what you may be thinking: avocado ice cream? How weird! Well, that's what I first thought too when I had something similar to this back in culinary school. I was a skeptic at first, but it's actually become one of my favorite refreshing ice cream choices in the spring and summer. The addition of coconut milk and toasted shredded coconut makes you feel like you're in the tropics while snacking on this avocado-infused dessert.

Prep Time: 10 minutes
Total Time: 2 hours 30 minutes (including freezing time)
Serves: 6 to 8

2   Hass avocados
1   14-ounce can coconut milk
½   cup heavy cream
½   cup sugar
1   teaspoon lemon extract
    Toasted coconut (see Tip), for garnish

Cut each avocado in half lengthwise. Remove the pit from the avocado and discard. Remove the avocado from the skin and transfer the avocado flesh to the bowl of a food processor or blender. Add the coconut milk, heavy cream, sugar, and lemon extract to the food processor and blend for 2 minutes, until completely smooth.

Transfer the mixture to an ice cream maker and churn for 20 to 30 minutes, according to the manufacturer's directions.

Remove the churned ice cream from the ice cream maker and transfer to a freezer-safe container. Cover and freeze the ice cream for at least 2 hours or until you are ready to serve.

Serve with toasted coconut on top.

Tip: There are two ways to toast coconut. To toast coconut in the oven, simply spread some shredded coconut on a baking sheet, transfer the baking sheet to a preheated 325°F oven, and toast for 15 to 20 minutes, stirring every 5 minutes to ensure the coconut browns evenly. Let cool before using. To toast coconut on top of the stove, put some shredded coconut into a small dry skillet over medium heat and stir the coconut frequently until the edges start to turn golden brown. Once the coconut is mostly golden brown, remove the coconut from the skillet and let cool before using.

index

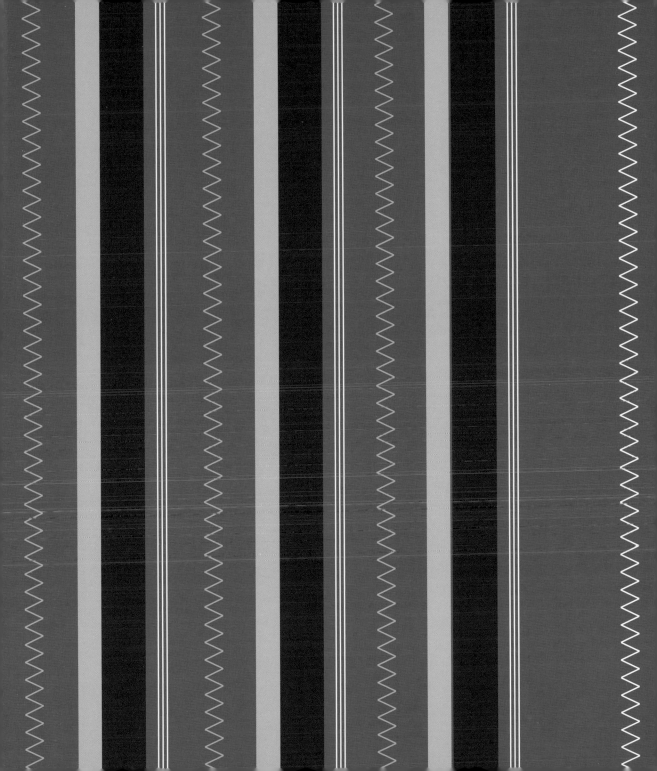